Sonnets

Stéphane Mallarmé

Translated by David Scott

With Introduction and Notes by
Mark Raftery-Skehan and David Scott

Shearsman Books
Exeter

First published in the United Kingdom in 2008 by
Shearsman Books Ltd
58 Velwell Road
Exeter EX4 4LD

www.shearsman.com

ISBN   978-1-905700-42-4

Acknowledgements

I am very grateful to my publisher, Tony Frazer, for the encouragement and expert assistance he has given me in producing this book; to my friend and colleague, the photographer Nicolas Fève, for permission to reproduce on the cover his work 'Blank Layout' (2004), an image that he tells me was in part inspired by Mallarmé's sonnet 'Le vierge, le vivace et le bel aujourd'hui', and which is now in my own collection; and, in particular, to my friend and IRCHSS scholar Mark Raftery-Skehan, whose inspiration and collaboration has enriched every aspect of this project.

Mallarmé

CONTENTS

Introduction

Stéphane Mallarmé (1842–1898) is among the greatest of the French poets, one whose relatively small *œuvre* has had a disproportionate impact on subsequent developments in theory, in the philosophy of language, and French poetry in the twentieth century. Essentially an occasional poet, Mallarmé's most original and successful writing was done in the 30 years between the later 1860s, when he underwent a spiritual crisis, and 1898 when he died at the age of 56. His writings can be divided into three main areas: the longer poems of his earlier period (1860s to 1870s, including *Hérodiade* and *L'Après-midi d'un faune*), his various theoretical reflections on poetry, theatre and music of the 1870s, 80s and 90s (in particular those gathered under the heading *Divagations*) and his sonnets of the 1880s and 90s which, along with his experimental poem *Un coup de Dés* of 1897, constitute his most original and successful poetic works. The thirty-nine sonnets presented here, with the originals and translations in parallel text, are in many ways his most typical and representative works in that they reflect a radical point of both continuity and discontinuity within a long tradition of European poetic expression and at the same time embody a uniquely modern synthesis of language's multiple potentialities.

In addition, Mallarmé's sonnets reflect an awareness of the elusive nature of poetic expression and a distinctively postmodern anxiety concerning the futility of representation in general. For Mallarmé, writing poetry was a complex undertaking, radically distinct from conventional uses of language. It implied an engagement with the universe, with the complex emotional and intellectual problems experience and/or existence presents to humankind and, most of all, the question of how phenomena and experience are represented through signs. Indeed, one could argue that for Mallarmé, the great metaphysical questions become enframed within a new consciousness, one in which the impossibility of metaphysical or total representation of the universe becomes both a given framework for poetic reflection and an object of poetic interrogation in his work. Poetry can no longer represent either the world or the poet's experience of it; instead it must produce a redeeming aesthetic that dwells on and revives a consciousness robbed of its pretensions and delusions with regard to providing a single totalizing signification.

For Mallarmé, therefore, in poetry, the *sign* as much as the object is at stake. Indeed, his finest poetry seems to reflect less on what an object or the universe is like than on the linguistic conditions which make representation possible and impossible, necessary and contingent. Mallarmé's concern with interweaving the tropic signifying capacity of objects and the materiality of the linguistic and visual signifier is evident in the play (as in the so-called *Sonnet du Cygne*) on the image of the swan (*le cygne*) which in French enables him to pun on *cygne/signe*. The swan is the archetype for the sign in that, singing only when it is about to die, it expresses the idea that the sign is born at the expense of the death of its object—by its very nature or at least according to its classical definition, as a sign bringing to presence something absent, and with which therefore it cannot be identical. As we shall see below, the translation of a poem, the substitution of one set of signs for another, or rather the substitution or transposition of signs from one integrated network into signs drawing their sense from another network, re-enacts at a further remove the drama of the substitution of sign for object or sign for sign. Additionally, the word 'sign', in English, enables a play on the anagram *sign/sing*—one which suggests that in substituting itself for its object, the sign, like the swan, *sings*, that is in some way lyrically transforms its object, idealizes it, metaphorizes it, by in some way articulating extra potentialities of meaning beyond and even in the absence of a literal or proper meaning. Taken to its logical extreme, this process leads to the *dissémination*—that infinite play of possibilities of signification, that process by which one signifier finds its signified to be but another signifier—that Derrida (1972), not least in reflecting on Mallarmé's writing, recognizes as fundamental to language as a system of representation.

Mallarmé's concern with the (post-)philosophical or semiological implications of the use of language means that his poetry tends simultaneously to operate on different levels: the recreation of intense aspects of experience (love or desire is a dominant theme), the hypothetical reconstruction of a plausible model of the universe (the metaphysical dimension), and an unending reflection on the nature of representation, in particular language (the semiological dimension). This leads to the density of Mallarmé's style and its relative difficulty: for the poet is trying to maintain a discourse that at once questions, illuminates and renders mystifying the bases on which it operates—as poetry, as language and as representation. Mallarmé's poetry is therefore as much about poetry and language as it is about metaphysics or love and invites a commensurate sensitivity on the part of the reader to the issues it raises. The reward for the reader is, however, more than handsome, for Mallarmé's poems seem miraculously to combine an intense lyrical celebration of an ostensible object—fan, hair, woman, sunset, universe—within a playful reflection on the nature of (representing) such objects or experience: in a sense it is not the least of the miracles of Mallarmé's poetry, as Jean-Pierre Richard, (1961) for example has shown, that these phenomena and tropic signifiers become analogies of each other—with a manipulation of the potentialities of poetic form that, while problematising language, at the same time takes its suggestive possibilities to new heights.

Another fundamental dimension of Mallarmé's concern as a poet is the problem of language as representation, in particular as it is expressed in the question of language and the page—that is, the non-representative space necessary to writing that ceases to be a figurative representation of empirical space. The blank space of the page or other tangible support, might be thought to have its correlate in speech in the abstract spacing or temporal pause that intervenes between the articulated sounds of spoken language. As a sign, the letter or the word is dependent on the space of its inscription, as well as on the space surrounding it that writing determines. The page as a space of representation and the interstices between words are of course in one sense anything but blank, for they articulate the determining relations in which words and textual units stand in relation to each other.

The *logic* of syntactical order to which western language is submitted (structured by phrase, sentence, punctuation) marks out space into conventional rational divisions that, in order to realise themselves, conjoin and differentiate textual elements and units from one another at different levels of the text (letter, word, phrase, sentence, and so on). The *blancs* thus testify to the demand that a given piece of language be referred to a radical non-presence within the text, that is, to the syntactical, grammatical and lexical conventions without which signifying units remain unrelated, illegible elements scattered across a surface.

Spacing is of course presupposed, its necessary presence and practice taken for granted and overlooked in everyday speech and writing. The determination of sense in and through the conventions of spacing make little or no impact on the conscious deciphering of meaning: the structural invisibility of syntax makes the blank form spacing assumes an apt but deceptive signifier. In poetry, however, such normally unconscious conventions of spacing and reading become freshly apparent because they find themselves incorporated into a *second* and analogous form of spacing and correlation, that of *prosody*. Mallarmé, perhaps more than any other poet of post-Renaissance Europe, heightened our awareness of *prosodic space*—the space of the verse line, of the stanza, of the various fixed poetic forms (such as the sonnet)—and of *prosodic logic* (rhyme, metaphor). In doing so, he calls into question that hidden prosody that underlines, supports and articulates regular prosaic language: the gaps between letters that enable letters to distinguish themselves as such by their spatial juxtaposition, the gaps between words that enable them to be identified as words within a syntactical chain, and the gaps between phrases and sentences that enable them to become quasi autonomous semantic units.

In attempting the ambitious project of restoring to the concept of writing the interaction between space and the written mark central to it, Mallarmé more than any previous poet, was thoroughly to exploit the relationship between the sonnet and the page or the *mise en page*. How does Mallarmé enable us to re-conceive of the space and spacing of the poem or text as something other than an initially indispensable but ultimately insignificant and non-signifying waste-matter or waste-product of reading comprehension? In a sense, he need only remind us that spacing is already availed of in the textual conventions which predetermine a page as a space prepared for representation, in, for example, the significant spacings that hoist and suspend the title, that punctuate paragraphs or stanzas (in particular that between octave and sestet in the sonnet) and that divide and conjoin lines of verse. Mallarmé's procedure is not simply an intellectual operation but an aesthetic and ironic one, in which he enlists spacing and all manner of *blancs* on the page to the cause. Mallarmé achieves the "reintegration" of space within the text and meaning by bringing the space of the poem's inscription fully and consciously into the signifying process; in other words, by bringing the page back into the forefront of the poem—as a process marking the inextricable relation between the *page blanche* that precedes inscription as its virgin space of representation, and as writing's condition of possibility, and the interstices and *blancs* that differentiate and syntactically conjoin elements; and by reminding us of the spatial as well as the linear (that is syntactical and propositional) logic that governs the creating of meaning in language.

This project reaches its fullest development in Mallarmé's spatial prose poem 'Un coup de Dés', but it is also fully explored through his use of more conventional poetic forms such as the sonnet. For the conventions of prosody—writing verse in equal measures or lines; vertically integrating lines into stanzas and poetic forms—create a space of reflection and suggestive silence surrounding the printed text that can aesthetically as well as semantically enrich the poem. The hierarchy of the sonnet's structure in which, as the poem develops, the language of each stanza becomes progressively more condensed, is thrown into relief by the stanza's interstices, these latter being pregnant with meaning, mute voices echoing the often unexpressed but implied transformations that take place from octave to sestet, from tercet to tercet. In the hepta- and octosyllabic sonnets to which in the 1880s and 1890s Mallarmé had increasing recourse, this pressure of the page is also felt laterally. The verses in Mallarmé's later poems come more and more to represent, as in the heptasyllabic 'Petit Air I' or in the octosyllabic 'A la nue accablante tu', brief and fragmentary gestures against the blank backdrop of the page. This explains Mallarmé's preoccupation with *les blancs* and the frequent recurrence of images of whiteness or blankness in his sonnets (the French *blanc* having a vaster array of significations than either 'white' or 'blank'). Meanwhile, the institution of a rhyme-scheme sets up a vertical logic of interconnection between words that enters into a dialectical relationship with the horizontal logic of syntax or proposition of the verse line. The effect of this is to open up and to spatialise the vectors of meaning-creation within the text, setting up tensions and enabling the discovery of unsuspected resonances between the words and lines of the poem.

And words in Mallarmé's poetry are always conceived as forms as well as meanings, acoustic sounds and graphic signifiers as well as signifieds. That is to say, the words of the poem are chosen as much for their sound or their appearance as arbitrary contructions in the differential system of language as for their meaning(s) (as signifieds). Indeed, a particular achievement of Mallarmé, allegorised in such poems as the *Sonnet en -yx*, is to show that poems are primarily constructions of words, feats of linguistic engineering rather than expressions of a pre-conceived meaning. This is because Mallarmé is conscious that the creation of meaning enters into a dialectical relationship with the formal or aesthetic requirements that are the poem's ostensible organising principle, the poem's form of itself already having meaning, just as a word's implicit *formal* as well as semantic potential is enhanced by its insertion in a formal context. So in the famous *Sonnet en -yx* (the first version of which dates from 1868, the final version—reproduced in translation here—from 1887) the necessity to establish a regular sonnet octave rhyme-scheme in two sets of four matching rhymes, in this case in '-yx' and '-ore' (a scheme that reappears in the sestet with its rhyme gender reversed to '-or' and 'xe'), justifies the quasi *invention* of the word *ptyx* to match the other three octave rhymes ('onyx', 'Phoenix', 'Styx') that complete the formal structure of the octave rhyme-scheme. So the as yet barely meaningful word 'ptyx' acquires sense through its insertion in the horizontal logic of the phrase; line 10 of the sonnet could be read as defining the word *ptyx* that immediately precedes it (line 9):

> Sur les crédences, au salon vide: nul ptyx
> Aboli bibelot d'inanité sonore
>
> On the console, in the empty room: no ptyx
> Abolished bibelot of sonorous inanity

—and in the *vertical* pattern of the rhyme-scheme which provides both its aesthetic justification (the completion of a set of four matching sounds) and a further dimension to its signifying function: connected with the other Greek-based words in 'yx', the 'ptyx' is part of a system of semantic connections that provide a basis for further, potentially infinite, patterns of meaning.

All this of course might appear as arid word-play were the completed texts not also able to provide the reader with intense aesthetic and emotional satisfaction. It is here that the role of age-old forms such as the sonnet and the guarantee of some sort of logic or sense that only syntax can provide ('Il faut une garantie—La Syntaxe—', *OC*, 1945: 385) together provide the framework within which the infinitely disseminatory potentialities of language can be to a certain extent harmonised if not controlled. Difficult though they may initially appear, Mallarmé's poems unerringly play on the expectations in the reader both of syntax or meaning creation and of formal or aesthetic completion or satisfaction, creating a tension and a challenge that is richly rewarded and indefinitely recreated with each re-reading of the poem. Poetic forms such as the sonnet that traditionally set up a high degree of formal expectation— exposition in the octave, resolution or transformation in the sestet—lend themselves particularly well to this sort of dynamic tension, while the fourteen lines of verse offer as many opportunities for the horizontal logic of the phrase to elaborate and complete itself within the pre-established limit of the poem.

Mallarmé's choice of the sonnet after the 1860s was due in no small measure to what he perceives as its absoluteness as a form:

> Immémorialement le poëte sut la place de ce vers dans
> le sonnet qui s'inscrit pour l'esprit ou sur espace pur
> (*OC*, Pléiade; Paris: Gallimard, 1945: 380).

For the sonnet's quasi immemorial origins that stretched back to the early Middle Ages, had conferred upon it a certain structural authority, one that allowed the author to be silent before a veil which disclosed only the articulation and pattern of the sonnet, declaring the form and order it brings to language and reflection. The 'absolute' fixity of form the sonnet provided allowed the poem to realize itself as an independent aesthetic object—a work of art as well as an inner life seeking expression; it allowed language rather than an author to speak, and the poetic ruse of necessity displayed in rhyme and measure to give to language's expression ideal aesthetic form. As its form began to crystallize, becoming for the Italians already more or less definitive with Petrarch in the fourteenth century, it was, thereafter, in Western Europe, something of a paradigm, eventually engraving itself, during the Renaissance, deeply into French and English sensibility and culture. It was no accident therefore that after about 1870, Mallarmé should exclusively adhere to two of the purest Renaissance sonnet patterns—the French abba abba ccd ede and the English or more properly Shakespearian abab cdcd efef gg. Mallarmé was the first French poet consciously to adapt this latter form (as in for example his 'Billet à Whistler'), although Baudelaire had already, without noticing it, written sonnets in this rhyme pattern.

But it was not only the prestige of a long and illustrious cultural history that made the sonnet irresistible to Mallarmé: it was also the absoluteness of its formal design. Already in 1862 Mallarmé had written to his poet friend Henri Cazalis:

> Tu riras peut-être de ma manie de sonnets [...] mais pour moi c'est un grand poème en petit: les quatrains et les tercets me semblent des chants entiers, et je passe parfois trois jours à en équilibrer d'avance les parties, pour que le tout soit harmonieux et s'approche du Beau.
> (*Correspondance*, 1959, I, x, 32).

In addition, the sonnet possessed a quality of variability within unity which seemed to make it the inevitable choice of a poet attempting, like Baudelaire and Gérard de Nerval before him in the nineteenth-century French tradition, to impose order on the tensions and antitheses that characterize the modern, post-Romantic sensibility. Thus, whereas for Nerval, the sonnet's elaborate framework, through contrast and juxtaposition, then fusion and final positive, if obscure or even mystical assertion, was able to structure the chaos of a complex inner life, for Mallarmé, after 1868 (the date of the composition of the first version of the 'Sonnet en -yx'), the sonnet was to become the compact theatre in which was enacted the philosophical and emotional drama of ideas and feelings and the problem and celebration of their ultimate indecipherability. For the quatrains and tercets, the individual unity of which Mallarmé stressed in the passage just cited, became for him steps in a poetic argument which, stage by stage in the quatrains, provisionally rejects and abolishes objects of the material world as such in order to establish an alternative hypothesis which transcends them by making of them signifiers. So when in 'Variations sur un sujet', Mallarmé describes the linguistic process as he understands it, he is also describing what happens in his sonnets:

> A quoi bon la merveille de transposer un fait de nature en sa presque disparition vibratoire selon le jeu de la parole, cependant: si ce n'est pour qu'en émane,

sans la gêne d'un proche ou concret rappel, la notion pure.

> Je dis: une fleur! et hors de l'oubli où ma voix relègue aucun contour, en tant que quelque chose d'autre que les calices sus, musicalement se lève, idée même et suave, l'absente de tous bouquets
> (*OC*, 368).

The sonnet lends itself particularly well to this sort of transposition or transformation, one in which the form's paradoxical capacity, as a compact and 'fixed' form, to open up the disseminatory potentialities of meaning within language, comes to the fore. So, for example, the *'Sonnet en -yx'* ('Ses purs ongles . . .'), illustrates Mallarmé's attempt to make Rhyme both the poem's compositional point of departure and to make the vain search for the extra, non-existent masculine rhyme in -yx reverberate in potentially infinite possibilities of meaning. If the rhyme scheme is completed here, it is only because of the capacity of the sonnet to position words syntactically, grammatically and contextually within a framework that compellingly invites the text and reader to confer on, or infer a sense for, the 'pytx', the 'Aboli bibelot d'inanité sonore'. The poem pretends to re-enact, ironically, the elusive unification of word and meaning, signifier and signified, the very creation of meaning in language. Here, poetry and language peer into the very conditions that make them undeniable empirical realities but also make them incapable of pure re-presentation. It is no accident, then, that the earlier, 1868 version of the poem was entitled 'Sonnet allégorique de lui-même—'Sonnet allegorical of itself'.

In this poem, not only did Mallarmé choose the most difficult rhyme-scheme imaginable but also, as we saw, in the process, found himself obliged to invent a word to complete it. Formal necessity thus enters into a fully dialectical relationship with semantic contingency, the ultimate aim of Mallarmé's sonnets being not a single meaning but Beauty, not straightforward discourse or assertion, but an 'argumentation de lumière' (*OC*, 385), in which images radiate or gesture towards rather than state their meanings or hypothesise on the process of meaning creation. In other words, the poetic process manifests an acute attention to—and retracing of the movement of—signifier to signified, of form to meaning, the endless retraced and arrested movement being that which is beautiful, or at least that which opens up the possibility of aesthetic experience.

Before proceeding finally to comment on the challenges Mallarmé's poetry raises for the translator, it might be helpful to give a sense of how the various motives governing his approach to poetic creation, and the ambiguities inherent in them, come together in a specific sonnet. We take by way of example a sonnet of the 1880s, 'Victorieusement fui le suicide beau', one that both continues and transforms the nineteenth-century French tradition of the sonnet as celebration both of the nature of the universe and of the loved woman's hair.

Whereas in the early part of the sonnets of *Les Fleurs du Mal*, the collection of Mallarmé's predecessor Charles Baudelaire (1821–1867), the poet usually names and identifies the reality he subsequently submits to metaphorical transformation, Mallarmé seldom does this. Instead, he plunges his readers straight into a metaphorical world, leaving it to them to deduce from the imagery the possible sources in experience of the development elaborated in the poem. Mallarmé does so not simply out of obscurantism or a perverse desire to disconcert, but because for him nothing is stable in the world so that the world of linguistic recreation, the world of metaphor, can be as 'real' and authentic as that outside. Indeed, both are mere representations, the world being indistinguishable from its linguistic articulation. For Mallarmé, the world of matter was arbitrary: it had no meaning until one was invested in it by human consciousness and imagination, or in other words by human representation. So whereas Baudelaire, making the assumption that pre-linguistic experience can in some way be shared, might have said: let's discover and explore the metaphorical significance of a shared experience of reality, Mallarmé says: let's rediscover and, if necessary, reconfigure reality in terms of the imaginative and metaphorical displacements language performs.

Like many modern abstract artists, Mallarmé, after 1870, seldom gives titles to his sonnets: their theme and meaning have to be discovered or created by the reader. How then do we deduce that what Mallarmé seems to be evoking in terms of a victoriously postponed suicide in the first quatrain of the sonnet is in fact a spectacular sunset? We do so by taking a general view of the quatrain's imagery, seeing what images, formally or thematically, seem to attract each other, what resonances they activate in our memory and imagination, and by reconstructing a (for us) imaginary scenario which may have some bearing on that perceived or imagined by the poet. Thus, already we see here activated the process of translation, one whereby the reader hypothesizes a possible sense or co-ordination of the images on the basis of which he may surmise or perhaps even forego ascertaining an authorial intention for the poet. In this way, it is language and the poem that *mean*, the poet receding from view: this is all the more the case in the compressed, elliptical and suggestive form the sonnet assumes. Thus the glorious firebrand, the frothing blood, the gold, the tempest (translated here as a 'gorgeous conflagration'), the crimson about to manifest some royal gesture in the distance, together plausibly suggest a sunset over water.

This hypothesis is strengthened by *intertextual* influences: we know for example that Baudelaire, much read and admired by Mallarmé, had thirty years before in his poem 'Harmonie du soir' evoked a sunset in terms of a gory drowning. Additionally, other evocations of sunsets in Mallarmé's own poetry also strengthen the plausibility of reading this quatrain in a similar way. The sunset was, moreover, one of the great commonplaces in nineteenth-century French poetry (as it was in the paintings of the period from Turner to Monet) and poets found it, as a theme, an irresistible challenge—not because it was a commonplace but because it encouraged them to explore its metaphorical potential in *uncommon* ways. Poets—Victor Hugo, Baudelaire and Paul Verlaine as well as Mallarmé—strove to overcome the despair and metaphysical anguish felt at sunset by the creation of some striking metaphorical transformation that would salvage the essence of the dying reality and refer it, without purporting to invest in it or affix to it a definitive, literal significance, to some more permanent or indestructible image within a metaphorical chain.

So, in Mallarmé's sonnet, the last flickers of the sunset are picked up by the pinkish blond hair of his mistress Méry Laurent where they become the nexus of a series of further metaphorical transformations that it is the function of the rest of the sonnet to chart, in a process of dissemination that affords subsequent literary criticism the infinite pleasure of attempting to retrace. So, for example, it may be hypothesized that the qualities of the dying sun ('or', 'beau') are transferred to the woman's hair, described as 'très-or' (very gold, treasure) and as being ablaze without flame ('sans flambeau'). The idea of the sumptuousness of the hair is embedded in the idea of its presumptuousness ('présomptueux'): the hair presumes with its own golden locks to replace and outshine the cosmic glory of the setting sun. This hyperbole of course relates Mallarmé's sonnet to a long European tradition of idealizing love poetry which dates back at least as far as Petrarch. Meanwhile, the 'beau / flambeau' rhyme is a nineteenth-century commonplace, already exploited, for example, by Baudelaire in love sonnets such as 'Le Flambeau vivant'. What is new here, as Richard (1961) has noted, is the effect that this enchaining, evolution and transfiguration of images into one another, and the recurrence of certain polysemantic words, objects or *thèmes* (*blanc, pli, éventail, néant,* etc.) has on the universe created or recreated in Mallarmé's corpus: it appears as an integrated and complex whole, invisible to a literal or empirical gaze or discourse, and whose links and unity poetry detects and creates by a metaphorical realization of the world in language.

The first tercet of the sonnet recapitulates and confirms the metaphorical transformation that the octave has achieved in relation to the sun / hair image and celebrates it with jubilant lyricism. 'Délice' has replaced thoughts of 'suicide' and the mistress's hair has succeeded in retaining from the fading sky 'un peu de puérile triomphe' which replaces the 'gloire' of Quatrain 1. Tercet 2 amplifes the vision of the 'trésor présomptueux de tête' of Quatrain 2: when its highlights ('clarté') are rested against cushions, like the warlike helmet of an imperial infanta, its final triumph will be figured by falling roses. So, this final tercet succeeds in synthesizing in an ambiguous but unforgettable image the elements of royalty ('impératrice'), victory ('guerrier', 'roses'), light ('clarté') and charming naivety ('enfant') which, for Mallarmé, make up the image of the mistress's hair and endow it with the power of transcending and superseding the images of suicide, death and despair provoked by the initial image of the dying sun.

This tercet is also a triumph of metaphor which asserts its autonomy and its ultimate undecidability in decisive terms: what are these roses that fall?—are they the flowers showered over the imagined returning victors? Are they the roses on the chinz-covered sofa against which his mistress is reclining? Are they the pink (rose) reflections of her hair against the satin of the cushions on which she is resting her head? These questions are not answered by the poet whose main function is to set up structures within which metaphor and the ambiguity of language can operate with maximum suggestiveness and autonomy. The text operates thus as a structure that invites the reader to explore his or her own experience in relation to the signs and images proposed, a re-exploration that may include reference to a shared poetic and literary tradition or *intertext*. In this way, the poem is endlessly completed by its reading yet harbours non-definitive, successive and differentiated reiterations, amongst which must be counted any proposed translation. Translation, in its broadest sense, will not, then, have been a supplementary version added to the original, but a transfiguration already potentially operative in the poem.

The horizontal logic of the successive stages of the exposition of the metaphorical potential of the object in this sonnet is complemented and enriched by the *vertical* vector of meaning-creation guaranteed by the sonnet rhyme-scheme. Indeed, the rhyme-scheme becomes a telegrammatic statement of the poem's theme: How can the poet convert a beauty, a *beau* which rhymes with death, *tombeau*, into life and delight? He can do so by taking a shred of cosmic beauty, *lambeau*, and by transferring it to an object ablaze without flame, *sans flambeau*. The *tempête* of Quatrain 1 is replaced by a *fête* and a *trésor présomptueux de tête* in Quatrain 2. In the sestet, the idea of the hair is embedded in the rhymes *coiffant* and *casque guerrier d'impératrice enfant* and the idea of ultimate beauty in the final rhyme of the poem—*roses*, here a symbol of both victory and desire. So, the different structures that constitute the poem—stanza, rhyme-scheme and syntax—are all mobilised in accordance with the demands of the metaphorical transformation of the fundamental image which informs even that part of the poem (Quatrain 1) from which it is absent.

The role of vertical as well as horizontal axes of meaning creation in the sonnet obviously makes it particularly challenging to the translator who is obliged to attend both to the linear logic of the phrase as expressed in the verse line and the spatial or tabular logic of the poem's overall profile. The sonnet translator's task depends thus on a double awareness: one that is syntactical and semantic as well as spatial and aesthetic. It is essential that a balance between these conflicting demands be maintained since the sonnet is essentially an expression of their dialectical interaction. The rhyme-scheme becomes therefore potentially both the salvation and damnation of the translator, as much perhaps as it brings to prominence the possibilities of language rather than authorial choice or intentionality. Operating within poetry's aesthetic response to the demand for a proliferation of sense, rhyme makes language and the sonnet rather than the poet the imaginative and creative engine generative of its meanings.

Just as the nineteenth-century French sonnet was often conceived primarily around its rhyme-scheme (as we saw, this point is made specific by Mallarmé in his '*Sonnet en -yx*'), only subsequently to be synchronised with the propositions extended by the verse line, so the translator has to reflect on the vertical and spatial as well as the horizontal equivalences of the target text. The translation must respond to the demand, a demand we will formalise shortly, for a prosodic and a semantic translation. In the event, the rhyme-scheme often comes to the rescue of the translator having difficulty finding an adequate equivalent for a word in the line; the legitimate demands of the rhyme-scheme may enable him to substitute or modify a semantic element in the line which would otherwise have given him difficulty. The translated poem must be, as we shall see, just that, a poem, an aesthetic object subject to the rigours and orderliness elicited in language by the sonnet. So, for example, in the translation of 'Victorieusement fui . . .', the poet's mistress is imagined to rest her head against a screen rather than against cushions so that the word 'screen' can rhyme with 'queen', a rhyming pair which also justifies the substitution of 'infant queen' for 'infant empress'.

The spatial dimension to poetry in general and to Mallarmé's sonnets in particular also justifies a pictorial or tabular approach to supplement the linear translation of the poem. The text is envisaged as a whole scenario in which various details may—in most cases will have to—be modified to accommodate the dialectical interaction of signifying vectors operative in the poem. Very often, the translation process as experienced here is one in which a landscape, setting or scenario in the poem is given slightly greater visual definition to compensate for some of the nuances that are lost in word-for-word translation. In other words, the translator here has, to a certain extent, defined certain visual features more specifically or, as it were, moved the furniture of the scenario around with the aim of recreating a more clear-cut image of the scene. The price to be paid for this no doubt presumptuous clarification is a certain reduction of the original's suggestive potential.

So in Quatrain 2 of 'Le Tombeau de Baudelaire', the unspecified gas-lit scenario into which the prostitute flits is defined as a park, not only so that a rhyme could be found for the 'lamp-post's arc', but also to provide a plausible setting for Baudelaire's marble bust and a scene for 'past opprobrium and unsettled score'. Another likely scenario, given the presence of the poet's ghost, might have been the graveyard where Baudelaire is buried (Père Lachaise in Paris), but the gas-light and the presence of the prostitute made this hypothesis somewhat less convincing. Similarly, in the 'Petit Air I', the virtually untranslatable 'gloriole' becomes 'belvedere', an image which strengthens the maritime or sea-port setting of the poem, as well as establishing an intertextual link with comparable poems in the work of Mallarmé's great immediate predecessor, Baudelaire (as in his prose poem 'Le Port'). In 'Billet à Whistler', the winds that blow along the street are more specifically identified with Chelsea where Whistler had his studio and where the gusts from the adjacent river Thames can be felt. In the translation of 'Une dentelle s'abolit' the draught flowing through the open casement causes the lace curtains to 'billow' ('s'abolit'), a (mis-) translation that heightens the visual effect of the image—the curtain, like the pregnant belly evoked later in the poem, swells outwards, while the 'b', 'l' and 'o' sounds of 's'abolit' are picked up by 'billows', reinforcing the words' aural equivalence.

Any rendition of a Mallarmean sonnet performed here can both mask and bear witness to the unenviable role of final adjudicator or arbiter the sonnet translator must assume (only one version or rendition being allowed) as well as the indecisiveness that may haunt both the translator's understanding and translation of the poem. If we formalise the impossible and congenitally irreconcilable demands the translator of the poem or sonnet is faced with balancing, harmonizing and appeasing, we find at least three worthy of mention, which we distinguish and enumerate here artificially given that they find themselves in play at any given moment in a sonnet's translation: the need to produce a work that is as much as possible an aesthetic whole in the target language and in its own right; the need to reflect the semantic, etymological, tropic nuances at the base of the poem's disseminatory possibilities in the original language in the target language; and the need to perform a faithful prosodic translation in which the finesse and complexity of the rhyme scheme and measure re-emerges in the translation. Each of them an impossible demand in its own right, acting in unison, they are sufficient to remind the translator of the futility and arbitrariness of his task.

The first demand above is in essence in contradiction with itself. For were one to produce an entirely new and independent aesthetic object, it would no longer be a translation as such. Here, the limits between translation and parody or plagiarism, those 'translations' that, respectively, are deliberate distortions or that go unacknowledged as such appear; or rather, the very limits that guarantee the possibility of translation disappear. In responding to the need to translate both vertical and horizontal axes, the translator must draw on his own imagination and the conventions of poetry in his own language in order to translate; more than one type of translation being in play—the linguistic translation and the translation into another aesthetic object, the translated poem is a transfigured configuration, a reconfiguration that must betray so as to be true to the original as a work of art rather than as language.

The second demand is no less paradoxical in that translation must first recognise the irreducible difference operative between languages before knowingly attempting a provisional, imperfect synthesis or reconciliation. Mallarmé's playfulness with the acoustic (homonymic), semantic, syntactical and logical aspects of the French language could never admit of adequate expression in another language. And on those occasions where, by the grace of equivalent resources in the target language, the target language presents analogous ambiguities or ambivalences, often, the rhyme scheme, measure (the third demand above) or simply the unnaturalness of the expression in question (the first demand) rule out its satisfactory employment. Thus for example, in the 'Sonnet en -yx', the final line, 'De scintillations sitôt le Septuor', translated as 'Presto! the glittering stars of the Septuor', would have admitted of alternative translations arguably more faithful to the French. The line is not 'Scintillations du Septuor', and it would be possible to provide a lengthy commentary on Mallarmé's use of the word sitôt here. For in the first place, in suggesting at once both the identity of the constellation with itself or the stars, it also paradoxically suggests the lack of identity and the anthropomorphism involved in naming constellations, or, in other words, the arbitrariness integral to the conventional framework by which constellations are named according to a perceptual superimposition of the conventionalities of figurative depiction and form, as in the case of the Plough. In a poem where the literal never encumbers the potentialities and hypotheses suggested by the images, and the vague yet suggestive logic that refers and transfigures the images into one another and thus that at the least promises to unite them, it is precisely this question or play of identity and non-identity, of signifier and signified, of positing and substitution, that the *sîtot* seems to reaffirm; and it does so even in the final, resounding last line where a definite image—and one moreover that transfigures the image of the stars in the first line from the hand of *Angoisse* they signified or personified to a redemptive aesthetic constellation—seems to bring the poem to a fitting and victorious climax. Thus, certain other translations presented themselves, amongst them, 'Presto! glittering stars or the Septuor'. Here, through this use of the word 'or'—which commends itself also on account of its French or Mallarmean resonances (see Derrida's analysis, 1972)—in the sense of 'in other words' or 'which we also call', it might have been possible to preserve the ambivalent logic at stake in the use of 'sitôt'. And yet, it is not altogether certain that the 'or' would in English be determined in this way, and certainly, the line loses some of its power to provide the poem with what might be interpreted as its definitive image. Translation thus simultaneously overdetermines and underdetermines, Derrida has said: this seems to us nowhere more apparent than in the translation of Mallarmé.

The demands enumerated above are intimately related to the synthesis of the vertical and horizontal axes integral to the production of a sonnet's translation. But it is perhaps the third of the demands regarding the production of a prosodic translation that relates most intimately to this synthesis of the vertical and horizontal. The rhyme scheme can rarely if ever be replicated in a manner that would make the two schemes formally or aurally identical. Rhyme operates only on the basis of the contingent if ordered and sometimes explicable recurrence of rhyme-endings in a language. Recreating a rhyme scheme and rhyme endings capable of producing the imagery, themes, or reflection in the original requires a willingness to draw from equivalent resources in the target language, an initiative which demonstrates how the translation of poetry is an exercise in the translation of aesthetic possibilities and patterns in language rather than (as is often the case in the translation of prose) the translation of a pure semantic content or the preservation of an original *vouloir-dire*.

The opting here for a more articulated, some might say over-determined, approach to the translation of phrases in Mallarmé's sonnets, places this translation as a whole within a framework more disposed to a hermeneutic rather than a semiological understanding of the text. The hermeneutic positing that texts are decipherable through critical interpretation is arguably more attractive to the translator and conducive to translation than is the notion that semiological and textual play thwarts all critical endeavours to produce or exhaust the work's signification in the original language. Decidable senses are easier to translate than are cases of undecidability, where the poem seems to draw from (its) language a proliferation of plausible or fitting senses that make the notion or action of deciding between them irrelevant and futile. We mean, then, that Mallarmé's texts are taken, as a critic such as Jean-Pierre Richard (1961) would read them, as more or less clear responses articulated through a poetic appreciation of the world's capacity to signify itself tropically and otherwise than literally; as more or less determined 'solutions' to the problem of the meaning(-lessness) of the universe, a universe neither more nor less illusory than is the world that is created or recreated by our capacity to reinterpret and transfigure through language; and as a successful attempt to reproduce through poetic language an *univers imaginaire* in which the presence of meaning and phenomena—spiritual or material—can be discerned. Through a thematic reading of the French, Richard argues, it is possible to reconstruct a unified framework within which more or less definitive Mallarmean interpretation is in principle possible. Even if translation into another language is ruled out in principle because replication of the intertextual play between Mallarmean words and poems is impossible, hermeneutics does at least allow the translator to have a defined poem set within a determined intertextual context, an original version divested of ambiguity to which he can aim to be true.

Richard's approach of course runs contrary to that which a deconstructionist philosopher such as Derrida might take, one which he indeed deconstructs in his acute reading in *La Dissémination* (1972), of Richard's study *L'Univers imaginaire de Mallarmé* (1961). For Derrida, Mallarmé's poetry expresses the profoundly modern intuition that there can be no fixed meaning expressed in language which in its intrinsic metaphoricity and its unlimited suggestivity is unavoidably penetrated by the *dissémination* that Derrida analyses and explores in his work of that title. It would have been possible to write translations that retained more of the inherent ambiguity and undecidability of language as intuited by Mallarmé and theorised by Derrida. But such translations, which might in some cases have followed the French text more closely, would have been of more difficult access to the English reader, and would have produced texts that might in themselves have read less satisfactorily as 'English'. It is primarily for this reason, that a more discursive approach has been taken here.

In keeping with an approach that attempts both to clarify the sense and to repeat the prosodic mastery of the Mallarmean poem, the translator has tried not to let close attention to the overall or spatial configuration of the poem as a form, undermine the equally essential linear progression of Mallarmé's phrases as they inscribe themselves in the Alexandrine or octosyllabic (and occasionally heptasyllabic) verse line. The integrity of the line of verse consists in its relative autonomy and its syntactical interrelations with preceding and succeeding lines within the poem, and its vertical relations to other lines in terms of their measure and the rhymes which complete them. Mallarmé, as we saw, like many nineteenth-century French poets, constructs his sonnets so as to produce key memorable lines, many of which are detachable from their context and take on the status of epigrams:

Tel qu'en Lui-même enfin l'éternité le change
As at last by eternity into Himself he's changed

Donner un sens plus pur aux mots de la tribu
To give a purer sense to the words of the tribe

Rien qu'à simplifier avec gloire la femme
If only to simplify woman with praise

Toujours à respirer si nous en périssons
Always to breath in though of it we perish

The translator thus made sure that these lines would still be identifiable within the English versions of Mallarmé's texts, thereby guaranteeing that the reader experience the infinitely repeatable pleasure of happening on them.

Whatever the approach made in this set of translations, it seems to us that the task of translating Mallarmé in particular, and poetry in general, as a project in some ways defeated in advance, are issues illuminated and best discussed within the insights afforded by the Derrida/Richard dialogue. In this context, Richard's analysis of the interconnectedness of the metaphorical significations across Mallarmé's work becomes readily apparent. Through the retracing and calibration of the recurring signifiers in Mallarmé ('miroir', 'evéntail', 'pli', and so on) which seem to be analogies, metaphors and metonymies of each other (the 'pli' being reflected in the folds of the fan, the fan veiling and unveiling as with the mirror), Richard argues, the Mallarmean *univers imaginaire* can be re-cognised and realized. These rich, elusive, polyvalent, polysemantic words come to be recognized not as arbitrary constellations of meaning bound together by a material signifier, but rather as *thèmes* whose interrelated meanings, as coherent, insightful unities in themselves are not only interwoven in Mallarmé's texts but in fact ultimately guarantee its systematic coherence, the profundity of its penetration of the universe. Disclosing the interrelations between Mallarmé's *thèmes* reveals the textual field of reference, the *univers imaginaire* that arises from a tropic and poetic gaze rather than a literal or empirical grasp of the world.

If a poetic *univers imaginaire* is the product of the Mallarmean text, can this *univers* be translated, or re-appear in virtue of the resources in English? If, as we have said, translation consists in transforming a text that draws on the network of signifiers in one language into the signifying network in another, how is the translator to replicate the manifold meanings that can be ascribed to the appearance of, say, the recurring word *blanc* in Mallarmé's text? The impossibility of such an exercise is apparent if we imagine translation to perform the task of replicating the exact interrelations between the multiple internal signifiers such as *blanc*, not to mention the further tropic twists to which these senses are amenable. In the case of *blanc*, the conceptuality that covers the field of 'blank' and the colour white are not (always) distinguished, or at least are signified by the same signifier. Separate terms in English (white, blank, gap and so on) differentiate between senses that arise from the one signifier in French. The interrelations between these articulated senses in English are already thought or comprehended in French through the maintenance of the same signifier. Mallarmé's *univers imaginaire* is thus native only to French, and as such cannot but resist translation into another network of signifiers. The textual recurrence of a word, and particularly that of a plural Mallarmean *thème*, brings translation to the absolute limit of its possibility. Linguistic difference seems irreducible here.

For Derrida the problematic of translation is not exterior to the problems texts, and Mallarmé's texts in particular, pose in and of themselves. This is the point that divides Derrida from Richard: the original text does not translate into itself fully, possesses no intrinsic and absolute identity divorced from its form and its play; the poem is but the sum of its possible translations.

Derrida's response to Richard and to this recurrence of words in themselves ambiguous, reveals then more fundamental conditions prohibiting translation and why the Mallarmean *thème* or poem never translates into itself or achieves a containable meaning to be mastered. Derrida reminds us that the Mallarmean *thème*, if we are correct in calling it that, is never the simple presence of a controllable myriad of meanings in one signifier but an elusive game or intertextual play between the infinite referents a signifier capable of initiating several semantic lines of thought might signify. The Mallarmean theme is not by accident a vague but rich assemblage of meanings; its very elusiveness, its very capacity to bring into play several senses at once is what brings Mallarmé back to it, invites its theoretically infinite reiteration, and thus in effect, makes of it a recurrent *thème* within his work.

It is here that Derrida takes issue with the assumptions underlying Richard's thematicism. In Mallarmé's use of the *blanc*, where reference to a textual *blanc*, to the *page blanche* and to the blanks of syntactical spacing can be adduced, ('Le blanc souci de notre toile', for example), Richard's very notion of a *thème* and with it the very possibility of a thematic reading, find themselves menaced. Here the text folds over onto itself, signifies not some entirely other world to the text but the elements of the text that make it possible. Thus turning back upon itself and recognising the materiality, differences, and spaces that orchestrate it, the *blanc* signifies the point at which Mallarmé takes cognisance of the limitations of representation, limitations which affect the effective communicability of a content, but which are potentialities of poetry as writing and as art. This textual allusion to the forgotten conditions of its production, for Derrida, makes all the difference. For the auto-referential signification confuses the boundary Richard would like to draw between the text and its machinations and the *univers imaginaire* that Richard holds to be the signified product of this play. For Derrida, the *blanc*, like all tropic, semiological play, is but a textual machination, reference to the world being inscribed within this play rather than extricating itself from it. The *univers imaginaire* takes place in the space between the white page and the text inscribed on it and according to the rules of its play. It is not only the Mallarmean *thème*'s potential for textual auto-reference, for tropically signifying or drawing on chains of other blanks that figure in Mallarmé's poetry that enables such an interpretation; the very repetition, reiteration or recurrence of the *blanc* is indicative of a deep reflection on the ambiguity of the signifier *blanc* (and perhaps on signification itself) and a cultivation of its poetic uses. In this way, much is lost in a translation that is unable to observe the uniformity of a signifier binding senses that are clearly differentiated in the target language.

How much more must this be the case in the translation of poetry where imaginative reconfiguration according to the resources of the target language is required? It is the play between the senses of the word, the intertextual references that can on occasion enable us to draw plausibly on the entire range of meanings the word suggests in French and in Mallarmé that is lost. It is a word or phrase's interaction with its own possible senses, with the other words and expressions of the poem, with the prosodic elements (the semantic juxtaposition or contrast between two rhyming words, for example) that defies perfect translation. But this very impossibility of translation may also be instructive with regard to what defines Mallarmean poetic praxis. For is not what Mallarmé is doing exploring and putting to poetic and aesthetic effect, in Derrida's words, the textuality of the text? Mallarmé's task, the poet's task, becomes one of composing and integrating the resources of language—semantic, etymological, prosodic, aesthetic—and setting them to work, what is thereby definitively produced being a matter for the imagination within language as much if not more so than the individual reader or poet. Language, the signifying network, the comprehensible yet elusive relations between signifiers, always intervenes, is always in a state of intervention, intervening in the process of generating what the text means or might mean. Mallarmé lets the text and language intervene in the name of an aesthetic of the generation or regeneration of meaning.

So, the translation of poetry ends up substituting one configuration's potentialities for the potentialities of another. The desire to translate can be fulfilled only at the cost of a linguistic bargaining, a negotiation entailing regrettable but perhaps sometimes fruitful compromises, a simultaneous depreciation and appreciation of sense and semantic possibility. Translation can thus both fail to deliver possible disseminatory paths there to be explored in the original version, while also setting out on and introducing some that may never have presented themselves in the original language. Translation thus fails to set itself outside the play of language in which, in truth, it will have been originarily inscribed. How then are we to conceive of fidelity or authenticity as central to the translation of poetry? This movement—of translation and dissemination, or translation as dissemination—does not necessarily lose what is Mallarmean in Mallarmé, at least perhaps for Derrida. On the contrary, the exercise of translation is an act that embraces both Mallarmean language and language as understood by Mallarmé. In language or in the fate of a text, its interpretations and translations, dissemination is ineluctable. Thus one does not betray Mallarmé in translating him, liberally or otherwise, because of the futility of the attempt to be faithful, whether to a *vouloir-dire* or to the language of the poem in the original.

If this introductory essay and the notes that accompany the text are in a sense supplementary to the translation, they are nonetheless integral to the attempt to overcome the impossibility of translation and of translating Mallarmé. Their supplementary inclusion cannot entail justifying every translation, exhaustively or otherwise, or enumerating the possibilities that were considered and rejected. The introduction and the notes, which we can only hope to strike a balance between the need for infinite elaboration, justification and determination with the need for an economical and judicious selection that informs the reader how we have read the works, have been included on account of a broad set of aims: firstly, in the hope that they illuminate the reasoning that has produced certain translations and foregone possible others (every translation implying other, options not chosen), selected cases of this reasoning hopefully being representative of the philosophy of translation adopted here; secondly, so as to reveal the intertextuality enriching Mallarmé's text that is lost in non-uniform translations of Mallarmean terms, that is, to point out selected points at which the translation can lead the reader away from the original, such a movement not necessarily being a straying, illegitimate movement but one central to the creativity that arises from the transposition of the aesthetic and signifying network of a poem into a translated other, as we have argued. The translation of poetry entails a poeisis of translation.

Perhaps an important component of such a poeisis, like that of the last line of the sonnet or of the completion of a rhyme with its echoing in another word, is to create the illusion, if only temporary, of the adequacy or the semblance of necessity in the formulation arrived at, with the unstated knowledge that many alternative solutions might have been possible. The creation of the illusion of inevitability becomes therefore part of the translator's task, this inevitability constituting an essential part of the aesthetic and emotional satisfaction the reader derives from the text. Nothing can appear to have been left to chance in the sonnet or, for that matter, in its translation. So while translation cannot help but reflect the process of dissemination at work in all language, like poetry, it aims to create a semblance of necessity, to make its no doubt arbitrary choices appear fully justified in the given context. The extent to which a translation is able to signal, through irony or humour, its awareness of its own presumptuousness and of what is at stake in its engagement with the process, should only enrich the reader's understanding and enjoyment. And perhaps overall, the notion of process cannot be overemphasized: language, verse, poetry, theory, signification, translation—all are part of an ongoing system or series of interrelated systems in which the pleasure and satisfaction of engagement should be as rewarding as the arrival at any—necessarily provisional—point of completion.

For Clive Scott, *il miglior fabbro*

Sonnets

SALUT

Rien, cette écume, vierge vers
A ne désigner que la coupe;
Telle loin se noie une troupe
De sirènes mainte à l'envers.

Nous naviguons, ô mes divers
Amis, moi déjà sur la poupe
Vous l'avant fastueux qui coupe
Le flot de foudres et d'hivers;

Une ivresse belle m'engage
Sans craindre même son tangage
De porter debout ce salut

Solitude, récif, étoile
A n'importe ce qui valut
Le blanc souci de notre toile.

Toast

Nothing, this froth, virgin verse
To mention just the toasting cup
Like distant sirens in a troupe
Frolicking upright or inverse.

We sail, O my crew members,
With myself already on the poop
You in the bows slicing through
The storms of thunder and Decembers;

A fine intoxication urges
—Without fear of pitch or surges—
Me to stand and make this toast

Solitude, barrier reef, star
To whatever merits most
Concerns born of our blank white chart.

PREMIERS POËMES

PLACET FUTILE

Princesse! à jalouser le destin d'une Hébé
Qui poind sur cette tasse au baiser de vos lèvres,
J'use mes feux mais n'ai rang discret que d'abbé
Et ne figurerai même nu sur le Sèvres.

Comme je ne suis pas ton bichon embarbé,
Ni la pastille ni du rouge, ni jeux mièvres
Et que sur moi je sais ton regard clos tombé,
Blonde dont les coiffeurs divins sont des orfèvres!

Nommez-nous... toi de qui tant de ris framboisés
Se joignent en troupeau d'agneaux apprivoisés
Chez tous broutant les vœux et bêlant aux délires,

Nommez-nous... pour qu'Amour ailé d'un éventail
M'y peigne flûte aux doigts endormant ce bercail,
Princesse, nommez-nous berger de vos sourires.

PREMIERS POËMES

FUTILE REQUEST

Princess, anxious as I am to rival Hebe's fate
Which dawns on this cup as it's kissed by your lips,
I burn my energy though I'm but a poor oblate
Who'll never as a Sèvres piece display his naked hips.

As I am not your toy-boy or designer-stubbled mate
Nor your lipstick, nor provider of mawkish beauty tips
And knowing that your glance on me does rest of late,
Fair one whose hairdressers are divine goldsmiths!

Appoint me . . . you whose peals of strawberry mirth
Come together as a flock of tame lambs on the heath
Grazing lovers' vows and bleating with delight

Appoint me . . . so that Cupid as his fanlike wings unfold
Paints me playing my flute as I serenade the fold,
O princess I'll be shepherd of your smiles, alright?

LE PITRE CHÂTIÉ

Yeux, lacs avec ma simple ivresse de renaître
Autre que l'histrion qui du geste évoquais
Comme plume la suie ignoble des quinquets,
J'ai troué dans le mur de toile une fenêtre.

De ma jambe et des bras limpide nageur traître,
A bonds multipliés, reniant le mauvais
Hamlet! c'est comme si dans l'onde j'innovais
Mille sépulcres pour y vierge disparaître.

Hilare or de cymbale à des poings irrité,
Tout à coup le soleil frappe la nudité
Qui pure s'exhala de ma fraîcheur de nacre,

Rance nuit de la peau quand sur moi vous passiez,
Ne sachant pas, ingrat! que c'était tout mon sacre,
Ce fard noyé dans l'eau perfide des glaciers.

The Fool Chastised

Eyes, lakes brimming with joy at my rebirth
As other than the ham actor whose gesture mimics
As with a pen the vile soot of the oil wicks,
I've torn out a window in the stage-curtain's girth.

From my legs to my arms a swimmer false as clear,
In repeated leaps and bounds, denying the fake
Hamlet! it's as if in the waves, unsullied, I make
A thousand tombs into which to disappear.

Like clashing gold cymbal attached to angry fist
Suddenly the sun strikes my pure nakedness,
Mother of pearl fresh in its cool respiration,

Stale night of the skin when you passed over me
Not knowing, you wretch, that it was my consecration,
That grease-paint drowned in water's cold treachery.

RENOUVEAU

Le printemps maladif a chassé tristement
L'hiver, saison de l'art serein, l'hiver lucide,
Et, dans mon être à qui le sang morne préside
L'impuissance s'étire en un long bâillement.

Des crépuscules blancs tiédissent sous mon crâne
Qu'un cercle de fer serre ainsi qu'un vieux tombeau
Et triste, j'erre après un rêve vague et beau,
Par les champs où la sève immense se pavanne

Puis je tombe énervé de parfums d'arbres, las,
Et creusant de ma face une fosse à mon rêve,
Mordant la terre chaude où poussent les lilas,

J'attends, en m'abîmant que mon ennui s'élève . . .
—Cependant l'Azur rit sur la haie et l'éveil
De tant d'oiseaux en fleur gazouillant au soleil.

Renewal

Now sickly spring has sadly driven away
Winter, season of art serene, pure winter,
In my being that gloomy blood does temper
Impotence stretches with a yawn all day.

Misty white dawns grow tepid in my brain
Gripped in an iron ring like a tomb
As sad I seek a fine if hazy dream,
Among the fields where sap supplies the grain.

Then I fall sated with the scent of trees
And digging with my face my fancy's grave
Bite into the warm earth where lilacs thrive,

Abasing myself, awaiting boredom's ease . . .
—Meanwhile the Azure blue smiles on the hedge
Rousing birds to sing the sun's diurnal pledge.

ANGOISSE

Je ne viens pas ce soir vaincre ton corps, ô bête
En qui vont les péchés d'un peuple, ni creuser
Dans tes cheveux impurs une triste tempête
Sous l'incurable ennui que verse mon baiser:

Je demande à ton lit le lourd sommeil sans songes
Planant sous les rideaux inconnus du remords,
Et que tu peux goûter après tes noirs mensonges,
Toi qui sur le néant en sais plus que les morts.

Car le Vice, rongeant ma native noblesse
M'a comme toi marqué de sa stérilité,
Mais tandis que ton sein de pierre est habité

Par un cœur que la dent d'aucun crime ne blesse,
Je fuis, pâle, défait, hanté par mon linceul,
Ayant peur de mourir lorsque je couche seul.

ANXIETY

I do not come tonight to vanquish your brute flesh
That bears the sins of humans, nor to whistle
In your wild hair a sad but raging tempest
Rained down on you in boredom by my kisses:

I ask but of your bed a heavy dreamless sleep
Floating under unknown curtains of remorse,
And that you may judge, after your dark deceit,
You who, more than the dead, know nothingness of course.

For Vice that has my native breeding gnawed
Has like you marked me with its stale decay,
But while your breast of stone is still unthawed

By heart of ice that no crime's tooth can slay,
I flee, pale, defeated, haunted by my tomb,
Afraid of dying when I sleep alone.

LE SONNEUR

Cependant que la cloche éveille sa voix claire
A l'air pur et limpide et profond du matin
Et passe sur l'enfant qui jette pour lui plaire
Un angélus parmi la lavande et le thym,

Le sonneur effleuré par l'oiseau qu'il éclaire,
Chevauchant tristement en geignant du latin
Sur la pierre qui tend la corde séculaire,
N'entend descendre à lui qu'un tintement lointain.

Je suis cet homme. Hélas! de la nuit désireuse,
J'ai beau tirer le câble à sonner l'Idéal,
De froids péchés s'ébat un plumage féal,

Et la voix ne me vient que par bribes et creuse!
Mais, un jour, fatigué d'avoir en vain tiré,
O Satan, j'ôterai la pierre et me pendrai.

The Bellringer

While the bell offers up its clear morning chime
To the pure, profound and limpid morning breeze
Pealing out over the child who in order to please
Rings out an Angelus over the lavender and thyme,

The bell-ringer grazed by the bird which he awakens
Sitting sadly astride the stone that will tighten
The ancient bell-rope, as he moans verses in Latin
Hears peals from above as only distant tokens.

I am this man. Alas, desirous of night,
In vain pulling rope to ring out the Ideal,
But instead drawing down the feathers of evil,

My chords voice fragments only hollow and trite!
But one day, O Satan, tired of pulling the rope,
I'll remove the stone and string myself up.

TRISTESSE D'ÉTÉ

Le soleil, sur le sable, ô lutteuse endormie,
En l'or de tes cheveux chauffe un bain langoureux
Et, consumant l'encens sur ta joue ennemie,
Il mêle avec les pleurs un breuvage amoureux.

De ce blanc flamboiement l'immuable accalmie
T'a fait dire attristée, ô mes baisers peureux,
'Nous ne serons jamais une seule momie
Sous l'antique désert et les palmiers heureux!'

Mais ta chevelure est une rivière tiède,
Ou noyer sans frisson l'âme qui nous obsède
Et trouver ce Néant que tu ne connais pas!

Je goûterai le fard pleuré par tes paupières,
Pour voir s'il sait donner au cœur que tu frappas
L'insensibilité de l'azur et des pierres.

SUMMER SADNESS

The sunlight on the sand, O sleeping vixen
Warms in your golden hair a languorous lotion
And, consuming the incense of your fiery complexion,
Mixes in with the tears an amorous potion.

Of this bright incandescence, the immutable calm
Made you utter sadly, O my fearful kisses,
'We will never as one mummy be singly embalmed
Beneath the ancient desert that the palm-tree blesses'.

But your hair is a river, a slow and lukewarm shoal,
In which to drown without shudder the obsessive soul
And discover the Nothingness you have yet to know!

I will savour the make-up your eyelashes spatter,
To see if it can give the heart that you strike low
The insensibility of azure and of matter.

AUTRES POËMES

LA CHEVELURE VOL D'UNE FLAMME . . .

La chevelure vol d'une flamme à l'extrême
Occident de désirs pour la tout déployer
Se pose (je dirais mourir un diadème)
Vers le front couronné son ancien foyer

Mais sans or soupirer que cette vive nue
L'ignition du feu toujours intérieur
Originellement la seule continue
Dans le joyau de l'œil véridique ou rieur

Une nudité de héros tendre diffame
Celle qui ne mouvant astre ni feux au doigt
Rien qu'à simplifier avec gloire la femme
Accomplit par son chef fulgurante l'exploit

De semer de rubis le doute qu'elle écorche
Ainsi qu'une joyeuse et tutélaire torche.

Autres Poëmes

The Shock of hair like a flame . . .

The shock of hair like a flame at the far
West of desire, to outspread it sheath
Alights (like, say, a tarnished tiara)
On the crowned brow, its ancient hearth

But to hope that this cloud ungilded but living
The kindling of a fire deep down inside
The one and only one—will continue to glide
In the jewel of an eye, piercing or laughing

A tender and heroic nakedness betrays
She who moves neither finger nor gemstone
If only to simplify woman with praise
Can accomplish the feat with her head alone

Of sowing with rubies the doubt that will scorch
Like a joyous and tutelary torch.

EVENTAIL DE MADAME MALLARMÉ

Avec comme pour langage
Rien qu'un battement aux cieux
Le futur vers se dégage
Du logis très précieux

Aile tout bas la courrière
Cet éventail si c'est lui
Le même par qui derrière
Toi quelque miroir a lui

Limpide (où va redescendre
Pourchassée en chaque grain
Un peu d'invisible cendre
Seule à me rendre chagrin)

Toujours tel il apparaisse
Entre tes mains sans paresse.

MADAME MALLARMÉ'S FAN

With as a language
Only a fluttering of wings
The future verse will emerge
From its rarified lodgings

A courier bird flying low
This fan if it be such
The same that behind which
Some looking-glass may glow

Limpidly (there to redescend
As a trace of invisible dust
With each grain only in the end
Kindling in me faint disgust)

May it always be descried
In your hands so occupied.

EVENTAIL

De frigides roses pour vivre
Toutes la même interrompront
Avec un blanc calice prompt
Votre souffle devenu givre

Mais que mon battement délivre
La touffe par un choc profond
Cette frigidité se fond
En du rire de fleurir ivre

A jeter le ciel en détail
Voilà comme bon éventail
Tu conviens mieux qu'une fiole

Nul n'enfermant à l'émery
Sans qu'il y perde ou le viole
L'arôme émané de Méry.

FAN

Roses for a life less rigid
Will all the same interrupt
With a stroke white and abrupt
Your breath become frigid

But if my regular beat
Delivers the deep welt
This frigidity will melt
Into life's joy and heat

Dividing up the firmament
See how as a fan in your movement
You are better than a phial

Nobody sealing with emery
Without losing or rendering vile
The scent emanating from Méry.

FEUILLETS D'ALBUM

FEUILLET D'ALBUM

Tout à coup et comme par jeu
Mademoiselle qui voulûtes
Ouïr se révéler un peu
Le bois de mes diverses flûtes

Il me semble que cet essai
Tenté devant un paysage
A du bon quand je le cessai
Pour vous regarder au visage

Oui ce vain souffle que j'exclus
Jusqu'à la dernière limite
Selon mes quelques doigts perclus
Manque de moyens s'il imite

Votre très naturel et clair
Rire d'enfant qui charme l'air.

Feuillets d'album

Album Leaf

Suddenly in jestful appeals
Mademoiselle expressed intents
To hear me playing various trills
On my wind instruments

It seems that my fine attempt
Started in a pastoral place
Finds its point when I relent
Turning to look you in the face

For this breath that I exhale
Until the final bitter end
Modulated by my fingers hale
Is too slow to catch the sound

Of your most natural and clear
Laughter that charms the air.

REMÉMORATION D'AMIS BELGES

A des heures et sans que tel souffle l'émeuve
Toute la vétusté presque couleur d'encens
Comme furtive d'elle et visible je sens
Que se dévêt pli selon pli la pierre veuve

Flotte ou semble par soi n'apporter une preuve
Sinon d'épandre pour baume antique le temps
Nous immémoriaux quelques-uns si contents
Sur la soudaineté de notre amitié neuve

O très chers rencontrés en le jamais banal
Bruges multipliant l'aube au défunt canal
Avec la promenade éparse de maint cygne

Quand solennellement cette cité m'apprit
Lesquels entre ses fils un autre vol désigne
A prompte irradier ainsi qu'aile l'esprit.

Remembering Belgian Friends

At times and without any breath to inhale
All that decrepitude, the colour of incense,
As though furtive of itself and visible, I sense
The widowed stone crumbling fold by fold to shale

Floating or seeming not to let proof prevail
Except to pour forth as a balm time's patience
We immemorial few so blithe in the conscience
Of our friendship as unexpected as unfrail

Dear comrades encountered in the never banal
Bruges where dawn reflects in the sleepy canal
And where swans progress as their whim dictates

When solemnly this city taught me to comprehend
Whom among its sons another flight designates
Ready to migrate like a wing through the mind.

Sonnet

Dame

       sans trop d'ardeur à la fois enflammant
La rose qui cruelle ou déchirée et lasse
Même du blanc habit de pourpre le délace
Pour ouïr dans sa chair pleurer le diamant

Oui sans ces crises de rosée et gentiment
Ni brise quoique, avec, le ciel orageux passe
Jalouse d'apporter je ne sais quel espace
Au simple jour le jour très vrai du sentiment,

Ne te semble-t-il pas, disons, que chaque année
Dont sur ton front renaît la grâce spontanée
Suffise selon quelque apparence et pour moi

Comme un éventail frais dans la chambre s'étonne
A raviver du peu qu'il faut ici d'émoi
Toute notre native amitié monotone.

SONNET

Lady
      without too much ardour enflaming the curls
Of the rose which cruel or torn and weary
Even of the white coat whose purple it unfurls
To hear in its flesh weeping diamond jewelry

Yes without these dewy crises and the breeze
That passes nevertheless with the stormy sky
Anxious to bring I know not what space and ease
To the simple day-to-day of our amity,

Does it not strike you, then, that every year
In which is reborn of your brow the fair bloom
Suffices for me and for whomever it appear

Like a fan cooling the air in the room
And reviving only if need be with emotion
All our native and monotonous devotion.

SONNET

O si chère de loin et proche et blanche, si
Délicieusement toi, Mary, que je songe
A quelque baume rare émané par mensonge
Sur aucun bouquetier de cristal obscurci

Le sais-tu, oui! pour moi voici des ans, voici
Toujours que ton sourire éblouissant prolonge
La même rose avec son bel été qui plonge
Dans autrefois et puis dans le futur aussi.

Mon cœur qui dans les nuits parfois cherche à s'entendre
Ou de quel dernier mot t'appeler le plus tendre
S'exalte en celui rien que chuchoté de sœur

N'était, très grand trésor et tête si petite,
Que tu m'enseignes bien toute une autre douceur
Tout bas par le baiser seul dans tes cheveux dite.

SONNET

Oh so dear whether near or afar and so white,
So deliciously you, Mary, that I dream
Of some rare balm emanating with deceit
From some crystal vase in a darkening stream

As you well know, for me, now, for years
Your dazzling smile endlessly prolongs
The same rose with its fine summer that cheers
Past and future, to both of which it belongs.

My heart that in the night seeks to be comforted
Or to discover a dear name on you to confer
Is elated by that only whispered of sister

Were it not that, golden treasure and exquisite head,
You teach me quite another and ecstatic bliss
Spoken low in your hair with a single kiss.

CHANSONS BAS

I

LE SAVETIER

Hors de la poix rien à faire,
Le lys naît blanc, comme odeur
Simplement je le préfère
A ce bon racommodeur.

Il va de cuir à ma paire
Adjoindre plus que je n'eus
Jamais, cela désespère
Un besoin de talons nus.

Son marteau qui ne dévie
Fixe de clous gouailleurs
Sur la semelle l'envie
Toujours conduisait ailleurs.

Il recréerait des souliers,
O pieds! si vous le vouliez!

CHANSONS BAS

I

THE COBBLER

Nothing doing except for lice,
White lilies are nobler
And simply smell nice,
Unlike my good cobbler.

He'll patch up my pair
With enough leather weals
To lead me to despair
Of a clean pair of heals.

His hammer never holes
Welts with a rude nail
But strengthens the soles
And the wish to set sail.

He'll make complete shoes
If that's what you choose!

II

LA MARCHANDE D'HERBES AROMATIQUES

Ta paille azur de lavandes,
Ne crois pas avec ce cil
Osé que tu me la vendes
Comme à l'hypocrite s'il

En tapisse la muraille
De lieux les absolus lieux
Pour le ventre qui se raille
Renaître aux sentiments bleus.

Mieux entre une envahissante
Chevelure ici mets-la
Que le brin salubre y sente,
Zéphyrine, Paméla

Ou conduise vers l'époux
Les prémices de tes poux.

II

THE LAVENDER SELLER

Don't think, though lavender's blue,
That your prettily arched brow
Would dare to sell it to me now
As to a hypocrite who

Hangs bunches on the walls
Of absolute places like loos
For the belly that appalls
By being born to the blues.

Rather place it in the curls
Of that fine pubic hair
So that the flower smells,
Pamela, fresh as a zephyr,

Or, as first fruits to appease,
Infect your husband with fleas.

BILLET À WHISTLER

Pas les rafales à propos
De rien comme occuper la rue
Sujette au noir vol de chapeaux;
Mais une danseuse apparue

Tourbillon de mousseline ou
Fureur éparses en écumes
Que soulève par son genou
Celle même dont nous vécûmes

Pour tout, hormis lui, rebattu
Spirituelle, ivre, immobile
Foudroyer avec le tutu,
Sans se faire autrement de bile

Sinon rieur que puisse l'air
De sa jupe éventer Whistler.

Note for Whistler

Not inconsequential puffs
That blow along a Chelsea street
Lifting hats and furling cuffs;
But a dancer, indiscreet

In a whirlwind of muslin
Swirling in a foaming surf
Twirling hips and revelling in
Showing that which gave us birth

For all, except him, too too
Much, but witty, gay, intense
She blasts us with her tutu,
And without further offence

Laughingly fans the air
Raising her skirt to Whistler.

PETIT AIR

I

Quelconque une solitude
Sans le cygne ni le quai
Mire sa désuétude
Au regard que j'abdiquai

Ici de la gloriole
Haute à ne la pas toucher
Dont maint ciel se bariole
Avec les ors de coucher

Mais langoureusement longe
Comme de blanc linge ôté
Tel fugace oiseau si plonge
Exultatrice à côté

Dans l'onde toi devenue
Ta jubilation nue.

LITTLE TUNE

I

Some sort of solitude
With neither quay nor swan
Mirrors the ineptitude
Of my glance that is wan

Up here on the belvedere
From a dominating height
Where the heavens reappear
In the colours of twilight

But languorously lunges
Like a white blouse thrown off
As a wandering seabird plunges
Exultantly from aloft

Into an effervescent tide
Your dive, jubilantly nude.

PETIT AIR

II

Indomptablement a dû
Comme mon espoir s'y lance
Eclater là-haut perdu
Avec furie et silence,

Voix étrangère au bosquet
Ou par nul écho suivie,
L'oiseau qu'on n'ouït jamais
Une autre fois en la vie.

Le hagard musicien,
Cela dans le doute expire
Si de mon sein pas du sien
A jailli le sanglot pire

Déchiré va-t-il entier
Rester sur quelque sentier!

LITTLE TUNE

II

Indomitably must
In my hope's expanse
Have sounded up there lost
In fury and silence

A voice stranger to the cover
Or by no echo followed
The bird that is never
Twice in life heard loud

The wild musician's sounds
Fade to doubt or distress
If a worse sob rebounds
From my breast not his

So torn up he will stay
Abandoned on some pathway!

PETIT AIR

(GUERRIER)

Ce me va hormis l'y taire
Que je sente du foyer
Un pantalon militaire
A ma jambe rougeoyer

L'invasion je la guette
Avec le vierge courroux
Tout juste de la baguette
Au gant blanc des tourlourous

Nue ou d'écorce tenace
Pas pour battre le Teuton
Mais comme une autre menace
A la fin que me veut-on

De trancher ras cette ortie
Folle de la sympathie.

LITTLE TUNE

(WARLIKE)

By the fireside where I tarry
Glad though I keep them hidden
Breeches worn by the military
On my thighs start to redden

I await the due invasion
With the cross composure
Precisely of the stiff baton
Of the white-gloved drum-major

Erect with its tenacious bark
Not to beat the Teuton
But to give a warning stark
Now of an attack hard on

And to cut the nettle's sting
Desperate with sympathizing.

PLUSIEURS SONNETS

I

Quand l'ombre menaça de la fatale loi
Tel vieux Rêve, désir et mal de mes vertèbres,
Affligé de périr sous les plafonds funèbres
Il a ployé son aile indubitable en moi.

Luxe, ô salle d'ébène où, pour séduire un roi
Se tordant dans leur mort des guirlandes célèbres,
Vous n'êtes qu'un orgueil menti par les ténèbres
Aux yeux du solitaire ébloui de sa foi.

Oui, je sais qu'au lointain de cette nuit, la Terre
Jette d'un grand éclat l'insolite mystère,
Sous les siècles hideux qui l'obscurcissent moins.

L'espace à soi pareil qu'il s'accroisse ou se nie
Roule dans cet ennui des feux vils pour témoins
Que s'est d'un astre en fête allumé le génie.

Plusieurs Sonnets

I

When evening's shade menaced with a fatal ruling
Some old Dream, desire and feeling in my bones,
Fearful of death beneath a funereal dome,
It folded within me its indubitable wing.

What pomp, O ebony palace fit for a king
Where laurel wreaths writhe in their final home,
You are but vanity for which darkness atones
In the eyes of the hermit whose joy's prophesizing.

Yes, I know that to night's distant end, the Globe
Projects with a great flash the mystery untold
Through the dismal ages that occult it less.

Space like itself in expanding or receding
Unfolds in this anguish with weak lamps for witness
That a festive star's genius succeeds in igniting.

II

Le vierge, le vivace et le bel aujourd'hui
Va-t-il nous délivrer avec un coup d'aile ivre
Ce lac dur oublié que hante sous le givre
Le transparent glacier des vols qui n'ont pas fui!

Un cygne d'autrefois se souvient que c'est lui
Magnifique mais qui sans espoir se délivre
Pour n'avoir pas chanté la région où vivre
Quand du stérile hiver a resplendi l'ennui.

Tout son col secouera cette blanche agonie
Par l'espace infligé à l'oiseau qui le nie,
Mais non l'horreur du sol où le plumage est pris.

Fantôme qu'à ce lieu son pur éclat assigne,
Il s'immobilise au songe froid de mépris
Que vêt parmi l'exil inutile le Cygne.

II

Can the pure and lovely and lively new day
Tear open with a stroke of its ecstatic wing
The hidden lake beneath the ice slumbering
Haunted by glaciers of flights that did not stray!

A swan from the past, remembering, can portray
Itself grandly circling in a despairing ring
Above the region it was unable to sing
When of sterile winter set in the bright dismay.

Its long neck will shake off the white agony
Space inflicts on the bird that denies it any,
But not the icy ground where its plumage is caught.

Phantom assigning to this place its pure icon,
It is stilled by a contemptuous daydream that sought
To clothe in cold exile uselessly the Swan.

III

Victorieusement fui le suicide beau
Tison de gloire, sang par écume, or, tempête!
O rire si là-bas une pourpre s'apprête
A ne tendre royal que mon absent tombeau.

Quoi! de tout cet éclat pas même le lambeau
S'attarde, il est minuit, à l'ombre qui nous fête
Excepté qu'un trésor présomptueux de tête
Verse son caressé nonchaloir sans flambeau,

La tienne si toujours le délice! la tienne
Oui seule qui du ciel évanoui retienne
Un peu de puéril triomphe en t'en coiffant

Avec clarté quand sur les coussins tu la poses
Comme un casque guerrier d'impératrice enfant
Dont pour te figurer il tomberait des roses.

III

With suicide's temptation fled
In a gorgeous conflagration
What distant cosmic jubilation
My unfilled tomb bedecks in red.

What! of all this glory not a shred
Remains at midnight's festive gloom
Except, presumptuous, in a flameless room
The treasured beauty of a golden head:

Yours and only your blond profile holds
A trace of faded light the sky withholds
As triumphantly in childlike poses

You rest your burnished locks against the screen
The warrior helmet of an infant queen
Figured majestically by falling roses.

IV

Ses purs ongles très haut dédiant leur onyx,
L'Angoisse, ce minuit, soutient, lampadophore,
Maint rêve vespéral brûlé par le Phœnix
Que ne recueille pas de cinéraire amphore

Sur les crédences, au salon vide: nul ptyx
Aboli bibelot d'inanité sonore,
(Car le Maître est allé puiser des pleurs au Styx
Avec ce seul objet dont le Néant s'honore).

Mais proche la croisée au nord vacante, un or
Agonise selon peut-être le décor
Des licornes ruant du feu contre une nixe,

Elle, défunte nue en le miroir, encor
Que, dans l'oubli fermé par le cadre, se fixe
De scintillations sitôt le septuor.

IV

Its pure nails on high dedicating their onyx,
Anguish this midnight upholds like a torch
Many vesperal dreams burned by the Phœnix
Gathered by no urn in any cinerary porch

On the console, in the empty room: no ptyx
Abolished bibelot of sonorous inanity
(For the Master left to draw tears from the Styx
With this object claimed by the void's vanity).

But near the vacant northern casement, an ore
Agonizes perhaps according to the decor
Of unicorns pursuing a nymph in a rix,

She, like a cloud in the mirror, an encore
In which the frame's empty stage can fix
Presto! the glittering stars of the septuor.

HOMMAGES ET TOMBEAUX

SONNET
(Pour votre chère morte, son ami. 2 novembre 1877)

— 'Sur les bois oubliés quand passe l'hiver sombre
Tu te plains, ô captif solitaire du seuil,
Que ce sépulcre à deux qui fera notre orgueil
Hélas! du manque seul des lourds bouquets s'encombre.

Sans écouter Minuit qui jeta son vain nombre,
Une veille t'exalte à ne pas fermer l'œil
Avant que dans les bras de l'ancien fauteuil
Le suprême tison n'ait éclairé mon Ombre.

Qui veut souvent avoir la Visite ne doit
Par trop de fleurs charger la pierre que mon doigt
Soulève avec l'ennui d'une force défunte.

Ame au si clair foyer tremblante de m'asseoir,
Pour revivre il suffit qu'à tes lèvres j'emprunte
Le souffle de mon nom murmuré tout un soir.'

HOMMAGES ET TOMBEAUX

SONNET
(For your Dear Dead One, her friend 2 November 1877)

—'When sombre winter passes over forgotten wood and heath
You complain, O solitary captive of the threshold,
That this sepulchre for two in which our pride takes hold
Alas is weighed down with the lack of a wreath.

Without hearing Midnight ring out its vacuous chime,
A vigil entreats you not to misdirect your gaze
Before, seated in a chair with its ancient baize,
The last ember will light up my Shade in time.

He or she who receives this Visit must resist
Overloading with flowers the stone that my wrist
With difficulty raises with its depleted power.

Soul trembling to be seated by the welcoming hearth,
To revive me all I need is from your lips to borrow
All night long my name whispered with murmuring breath'.

LE TOMBEAU D'EDGAR POE

Tel qu'en Lui-même enfin l'éternité le change,
Le Poëte suscite avec un glaive nu
Son siècle épouvanté de n'avoir pas connu
Que la mort triomphait dans cette voix étrange!

Eux, comme un vil sursaut d'hydre oyant jadis l'ange
Donner un sens plus pur aux mots de la tribu
Proclamèrent très haut le sortilège bu
Dans le flot sans honneur de quelque noir mélange.

Du sol et de la nue hostiles, ô grief!
Si notre idée avec ne sculpte un bas-relief
Dont la tombe de Poe éblouissante s'orne,

Calme bloc ici-bas chu d'un désastre obscur,
Que ce granit du moins montre à jamais sa borne
Aux noirs vols du Blasphème épars dans le futur.

THE TOMB OF EDGAR ALLAN POE

As at last by eternity into Himself he's changed,
The Poet awakens with a naked sword
His century appalled not to have heard the word
That death was triumphant in this voice so strange!

They like a hydra hearing the angel's admonition
To give a purer sense to the words of the tribe
Noisily proclaimed the magic spell imbibed
In the dishonoured flow of some murky potion.

By hostile ground and sky he alas comes to grief
Unless our thoughts conspire to sculpt a bass relief
By which the tomb of Poe can his glory proclaim,

Calm block projected earthwards by disaster obscure,
Let this granite at least eternally disclaim
Any dark barbs of Blasphemy uttered in the future.

Le Tombeau de Charles Baudelaire

Le temple enseveli divulgue par la bouche
Sépucrale d'égout bavant boue et rubis
Abominablement quelque idole Anubis
Tout le museau flambé comme un aboi farouche

Ou que le gaz récent torde la mèche louche
Essuyeuse on le sait des opprobres subis
Il allume hagard un immortel pubis
Dont le vol selon le réverbère découche

Quel feuillage séché dans les cités sans soir
Votif pourra bénir comme elle se rasseoir
Contre le marbre vainement de Baudelaire

Au voile qui le ceint absente avec frissons
Celle son Ombre même un poison tutélaire
Toujours à respirer si nous en périssons.

A Tomb for Baudelaire

The buried temple divulges through the dark
Drain-mouth spewing mud and rubies
The sepulchral remains of some idol Anubis
Whose muzzle's ablaze in an abominable bark

Or the recently lit gas lights up the park
Scene of past opprobrium and unsettled score
And the ragged outline of some immortal whore
Whose flight is projected by the lamp-post's arc

What withered wreaths in cities without night
Could offer votive blessings as she would alight
Vainly against the marble of Baudelaire's bust

Whose Ghost, though veiled in absence, mournful, we cherish
As a poisonous yet tutelary dust
Always to breathe in though of it we perish.

TOMBEAU

Anniversaire—Janvier 1897

Le noir roc courroucé que la bise le roule
Ne s'arrêtera ni sous de pieuses mains
Tâtant sa ressemblance avec les maux humains
Comme pour en bénir quelque funeste moule.

Ici presque toujours si le ramier roucoule
Cet immatériel deuil opprime de maints
Nubiles plis l'astre mûri des lendemains
Dont un scintillement argentera la foule.

Qui cherche, parcourant le solitaire bond
Tantôt extérieur de notre vagabond—
Verlaine? Il est caché parmi l'herbe, Verlaine

A ne surprendre que naïvement d'accord
La lèvre sans y boire ou tarir son haleine
Un peu profond ruisseau calomnié la mort.

VERLAINE'S TOMB

The rock angry at being set rolling by the gale
Will not stop or be checked by pious hands
Feeling its likeness to the malaise of humans
As if to bless in it some cautionary tale.

Here as always if the ringdove coos loud
Immaterial grief with its myriad furrows
Oppresses the star with its long tomorrows
A gleam of which highlights the funeral crowd.

Who seeks, following the solitary lane
Prospected outside by the vagabond bard—
Verlaine? he is hidden in the grass, Verlaine

To be discovered only naively in accord
His lip not drinking and his lungs void of breath
In a shallow and much maligned stream called death.

HOMMAGE

Le silence déjà funèbre d'une moire
Dispose plus qu'un pli seul sur le mobilier
Que doit un tassement du principal pilier
Précipiter avec le manque de mémoire.

Notre si vieil ébat triomphal du grimoire,
Hiéroglyphes dont s'exalte le millier
A propager de l'aile un frisson familier!
Enfouissez-le-moi plutôt dans une armoire.

Du souriant fracas originel haï
Entre elles de clartés maîtresses a jailli
Jusque vers un parvis né pour leur simulacre,

Trompettes tout haut d'or pâmé sur les vélins,
Le dieu Richard Wagner irradiant un sacre
Mal tu par l'encre même en sanglots sibyllins.

Homage (to Wagner)

The silence already funereal of a pall
Disposes of more than one fold in the decor
Which the settling of the central pillar
Causes to plunge with its lack of recall.

Our ancient and triumphant revels in the tome,
With its hieroglyphs that enchant the many
Offering in its leaves thrills familiar yet uncanny!
Throw all that rather into some backroom.

From the exuberant racket initially offended
Among clear and masterly notes has descended
Onto the scene made for their simulating,

With golden trumpets blaring over their scores,
The godlike Richard Wagner in glory radiating
Sounds ink itself voices in sibylline encores.

HOMMAGE

Toute Aurore même gourde
A crisper un poing obscur
Contre des clairons d'azur
Embouchés par cette sourde

A le pâtre avec la gourde
Jointe au bâton frappant dur
Le long de son pas futur
Tant que la source ample sourde

Par avance ainsi tu vis
O solitaire Puvis
De Chavannes
                    jamais seul

De conduire le temps boire
A la nymphe sans linceul
Que lui découvre ta Gloire.

HOMAGE (TO PUVIS DE CHAVANNES)

Every Dawn however numb
Clenching a dark fist
Against bugles of amethyst
Raised to lips still dumb

Has a pastor with a gourd
Joined to the walking stick
Tapping his step, futuristic,
While the spring still poured

So ahead of time your life is
O Solitary Puvis
De Chavannes
                    never alone

That it leads time to hover
By the nymph without gravestone
That your Glory will discover.

AU SEUL SOUCI DE VOYAGER . . .

Au seul souci de voyager
Outre une Inde splendide et trouble
—Ce salut soit le messager
Du temps, cap que ta poupe double

Comme sur quelque vergue bas
Plongeante avec la caravelle
Ecumait toujours en ébats
Un oiseau d'annonce nouvelle

Qui criait monotonement
Sans que la barre ne varie
Un inutile gisement
Nuit, désespoir et pierrerie

Par son chant reflété jusqu'au
Sourire du pâle Vasco.

TO THE SOLE CARE OF THE VOYAGER . . .

To the sole care of the voyager
Apart from India's splendid scoop
This greeting is time's messenger,
Cape that's rounded by your poop

As if alighting on the boom
Plunging low with the boat
From skimming o'er the foam
A harbinger bird still afloat

Cries out in a monotone
Without any change of bearing
By the ship or in its rigging
Night, despair, precious stone

Its song reflecting the pale glamour
Of your smile, Vasco de Gama.

TOUTE L'ÂME RÉSUMÉE . . .

Toute l'âme résumée
Quand lente nous l'expirons
Dans plusieurs ronds de fumée
Abolis en autres ronds

Atteste quelque cigare
Brûlant savamment pour peu
Que la cendre se sépare
De son clair baiser de feu

Ainsi le chœur des romances
A la lèvre vole-t-il
Exclus-en si tu commences
Le réel parce que vil

Le sens trop précis rature
Ta vague littérature.

THE WHOLE SOUL SUMMED UP . . .

The whole soul summed up
When we exhale it slowly
In puffs of smoke wholly
Vaporized in other puffs

Attests a cigarette
Burning slow to inspire
Its ash not to separate
From its caress of fire

So the choirs of romance
Fly to lips that smile
Exclude when you commence
The real because its vile

A sense that is too terse
Will undermine your verse.

I

Tout Orgueil fume-t-il du soir,
Torche dans un branle étouffée
Sans que l'immortelle bouffée
Ne puisse à l'abandon surseoir!

La chambre ancienne de l'hoir
De maint riche mais chu trophée
Ne serait pas même chauffée
S'il survenait par le couloir.

Affres du passé nécessaires
Agrippant comme avec des serres
Le sépulcre de désaveu,

Sous un marbre lourd qu'elle isole
Ne s'allume pas d'autre feu
Que la fulgurante console.

Autres Poëmes et sonnets

I

Is every smoking twilight
Like a firebrand snuffed
With the immortal puff
Guarding no gleam of light!

The heir's old-fashioned chamber
Rich in fine but fallen trophy
Even came he by the lobby
Would not warm a dying ember.

The necessary pangs of yore
Clutching like a sharpened claw
Repudiation's pyre,

Sealed in heavy marble
Lights up no other fire
Than the shining console table.

II

Surgi de la croupe et du bond
D'une verrerie éphémère
Sans fleurir la veillée amère
Le col ignoré s'interrompt.

Je crois bien que deux bouches n'ont
Bu, ni son amant ni ma mère,
Jamais à la même Chimère,
Moi, sylphe de ce froid plafond!

Le pur vase d'aucun breuvage
Que l'inexhaustible veuvage
Agonise mais ne consent,

Naïf baiser des plus funèbres!
A rien expirer annonçant
Une rose dans les ténèbres.

II

Surging from the fragile womb
Of an ephemeral piece of glass
Through the long evening's gloom
No nativity comes to pass.

I think no mouths have been drinking
Neither my mother nor her admirer,
Ever at the same Chimera,
I, sylph of this cold ceiling!

The vase pure of all essence
Except eternal abstinence
Agonizes but will not consent,

Most funereal of kisses!
To announce or to present
A rose in the darkness.

III

Une dentelle s'abolit
Dans le doute du Jeu suprême
A n'entr'ouvrir comme un blasphème
Qu'absence éternelle de lit.

Cet unanime blanc conflit
D'une guirlande avec la même,
Enfui contre la vitre blême
Flotte plus qu'il n'ensevelit.

Mais, chez qui du rêve se dore
Tristement dort une mandore
Au creux néant musicien

Telle que vers quelque fenêtre
Selon nul ventre que le sien,
Filial on aurait pu naître.

III

A lace curtain billows
In view of Doubt's supremacy
Revealing as a blasphemy
Eternally virgin pillows.

This crisp and even conflict
Of white muslin with itself,
Is blown against the window-shelf
As a wan and soundless edict.

But he for whom a dream appears
Sad strains of silent music hears
From the hollow viol within

So that from a sash forlorn
A note of native sound in him,
Filial, might have been born.

QUELLE SOIE AUX BAUMES DE TEMPS . . .

Quelle soie aux baumes de temps
Où la Chimère s'exténue
Vaut la torse et native nue
Que, hors de ton miroir, tu tends!

Les trous de drapeaux méditants
S'exaltent dans notre avenue:
Moi, j'ai ta chevelure nue
Pour enfouir mes yeux contents.

Non! La bouche ne sera sûre
De rien goûter à sa morsure,
S'il ne fait, ton princier amant,

Dans la considérable touffe
Expirer, comme un diamant,
Le cri des Gloires qu'il étouffe.

WHAT SILK SMOOTHED BY TIME'S BALM . . .

What silk smoothed by time's balm
In which a fading Chimaera rests
Is worth the clouding native breasts
That from your looking glass you charm!

The holes of meditating flags
Bedeck our festive avenues,
But I have your hair's curlicues
To catch my glad eyes in their snags.

No! the mouth will not be sure
To fully taste its keen pleasure
If your prince fails to make expire

Muffled in the voluptuous tuft
As gloriously as a sapphire
The cry of Ecstasy that's snuffed.

M'INTRODUIRE DANS TON HISTOIRE . . .

M'introduire dans ton histoire
C'est en héros effarouché
S'il a du talon nu touché
Quelque gazon de territoire

A des glaciers attentatoire
Je ne sais le naïf péché
Que tu n'auras pas empêché
De rire très haut sa victoire

Dis si je ne suis pas joyeux
Tonnerre et rubis aux moyeux
De voir en l'air que ce feu troue

Avec des royaumes épars
Comme mourir pourpre la roue
Du seul vespéral de mes chars.

Let me come into your story . . .

Let me come into your story
As naked hero I propose
To mark with hesitating toes
The turf of native territory

As the sun's dying glory
Passes through an azure mist
Like a crimson-gloved fist
Raised in weary victory

Tell me if I may not hope
To escalate the virgin slope
Of a glacier's rosy crest

And view a landscape of desire
Where at last may come to rest
My only vesperal chariot of fire.

A LA NUE ACCABLANTE TU . . .

A la nue accablante tu
Basse de basalte et de laves
A même les échos esclaves
Par une trompe sans vertu

Quel sépulcral naufrage (tu
Le sait, écume, mais y baves)
Suprême une entre les épaves
Abolit le mât dévêtu

Ou cela que furibond faute
De quelque perdition haute
Tout l'abîme vain éployé

Dans le si blanc cheveu qui traîne
Avarement aura noyé
Le flanc enfant d'une sirène.

Engulfed in devastating cloud
And floundering on the oily brink
Of an echoing sea of ink
Closing over like a shroud

What shipwreck (foam, you think
You know, and trumpet loud)
Among disasters the most proud
Makes a broken topsail sink

Or that most fateful flaw
Perdition dealt by vessel's yaw
A whole abyss vainly deployed

In the foaming locks' long sigh
Greedily will have destroyed
A childlike siren's naked thigh.

Mes bouqins refermés sur le nom de Paphos . . .

Mes bouqins refermés sur le nom de Paphos,
Il m'amuse d'élire avec le seul génie
Une ruine, par mille écumes bénie
Sous l'hyacinthe, au loin, des jours triomphaux.

Coure le froid avec ses silences de faux,
Je n'y hululerai pas de vide nénie
Si ce très blanc ébat au ras du sol dénie
A tout site l'honneur du paysage faux.

Ma faim qui d'aucuns fruits ici ne se régale
Trouve en leur docte manque une saveur égale:
Qu'un éclate de chair humain et parfumant!

Le pied sur quelque guivre où notre amour tisonne,
Je pense plus longtemps peut-être éperdument
A l'autre, au sein brûlé d'une antique amazone.

WITH MY PAPERBACKS CLOSED ON PAPHOS'S NAME . . .

With my paperbacks closed on Paphos's name,
I like to conjure with my spirit alone
A ruin, blessed by tides of incoming foam
Beneath the distant blue of its days of fame

Let the cold water run from the murmurless main
I will not fill the void with a fatuous rune
If this incoming flow as it runs up the dune
Denies all sites the charm of an illusory frame.

My hunger which tonight no rare fruits favour
Finds in their learned absence a comparable flavour:
Let one at least burst open, human and fragrant!

My foot on the griffin by which our love's emblazoned,
I reflect in a manner desirous, even flagrant
On the other, the breast of a bronzed Amazon.

Thirty-nine Sonnets by Mallarmé: Notes

Of the total of forty-seven sonnets reproduced in the Pléiade edition (1945) of Mallarmé's *Oeuvres complètes*, thirty-nine are reproduced here, two early sonnets and six later ones from the *Vers de circonstance* being omitted.

Salut

Usually placed as a liminal poem in Mallarmé's *Poésies*, this sonnet of 1893, was also entitled *Toast*, underlying the three principle meanings of the word 'salut' in French: greetings (also wave, salute), toast, (good health) and salvation. As with other sonnets of his later period (such as the *Hommage* dedicated to Vasco de Gama), *Salut* produces one of those lapidary lines—'Solitude, récif, étoile'—that sum up for Mallarmé the condition, danger and aim of poetic creation. A toast ostensibly addressed to fellow poets ('crew members'), the poem draws on two domains of imagery dear to Mallarmé, gracefully mapping storm-tossed seas (and all the related phenomena and significance—the menace of the reef, the pitiable shipwreck, the lure and allure of the siren, seafaring as the metaphorical surrender of one's fate to the chance element of the sea, and so on) onto the auto-referential imagery of writing and the blank page, the point of crowning intersection coming in the last line—'Le blanc souci de notre toile'.

The ambivalence of the 'toile', of the white sail which awaits and subsequently relates to us that which we hold most dear, lies in its capacity to signify the heading and destiny of poetry as well as, or in and through, signifying the white page that confronts and enables the poem. In order to preserve this ambivalence in the absence of available rhymes in English, 'toile' was substituted by an alternative nautical image, that of the 'chart'. Such formulae demand close attention in the translation process, having to be salvaged with a desperation similar to that of any other fragment of the shipwreck of language that, for Mallarmé, is poetry.

'Salut' continues the questioning of the signification of a star, which for Mallarmé seems, in virtue of the diverse and arbitrary contexts that illuminate yet fail to exhaust its range of interpretations, to stand for the absence of any given, predefined literal or proper sense. For which reason, the poem aims to propose possible responses rather than a definitive empirical or conceptual meaning. In this way, as will often be the case with Mallarmean imagery, the purpose and delight of the image lies in posing the question of whether, among other possibilities, it signifies a salutary navigational heading or a non-life-giving sun that reflects the cosmic insignificance of man in which the *Néant* finds aesthetic redemption.

Premiers Poëmes

These sonnets dating from the early 1860s, reflect Mallarmé's precocious interest in the sonnet form—an interest anticipated in two even earlier sonnets, 'Sonnet' and 'Contre un poëte parisien' in *Poëmes d'enfance et de jeunesse* (not reproduced or translated here). The poems reflect the formal concerns and pastoral or circus imagery of the Parnassian poets, those who (as will be seen in the next section) contributed to the successive numbers of the journal *Le Parnasse contemporain* (1866, 1869 and 1876). The *mièvre* or preciously sentimental tone of these sonnets ('Placet futile', 'Le Pitre châtié') will disappear from Mallarmé's writing after the late 1860s.

The Baudelairian image of the window or *fenêtre*—as in Baudelaire's sonnet 'Le Gouffre' of 1861: 'Je ne vois qu'infini par toutes les fenêtres'—already emerges in Mallarmé's 'Le Pitre châtié' as an image of representation and, will later in the 1860s—as in 'Le Sonnet en -yx'—appear as a frame through which the infinite vastness of the universe is perceived. The image of Hamlet is another *leitmotiv* that will hover in the background of Mallarmé's reflection on the human condition from the 1860s through to *Un coup de Dés* of 1897.

In 'Placet futile', the image of the fan or *éventail* is one of those dialectical phenomena (*plume*, wave, spray or *écume*, cup or amphora, etc) in which the interplay between absence or a space and the matter of the object is central to their definition or function, all of which might be said to figure the spacing of writing and poetry and the dialectical interaction of beings and spacing. Such images will become central leitmotifs in Mallarmé's later poetry where they express a reflection on the poetic act and its problematic status in relation to meaning as well as on the fragility of the human enterprise in the infinity of the cosmic order. The fan as an image is also charged with a certain eroticism and thus is central in love poems addressed to women such as 'Eventail de Madame Mallarmé', 'Eventail', 'Sonnet', all of which appear in *Autres Poëmes*.

Le Parnasse contemporain

These poems appeared in the 1866 edition of *Le Parnasse contemporain* and reflect the style and content of other contributors to this volume—Théodore de Banville, Charles Baudelaire, José Maria de Heredia, the early Paul Verlaine. The influence of Baudelaire ('Angoisse', 'Le Sonneur') is particularly marked, the allusions to Satan, Vice and the Ideal, adding to the heterogeneity of the poems' imagery and to the corresponding difficulty of their translation.

Autres Poëmes

The poems in this section, dating from the 1870s to the 1890s, already show that Mallarmé reached a maturity, distinctiveness and sophistication in his poetic style that would last to his death in 1898. Although in the 1870s Mallarmé was still committed to longer poems—'Hérodiade', 'L'Après-midi d'un faune', 'Toast funèbre'—his mature style in subsequent decades is effortlessly applied to poems such as 'La Chevelure vol d'une flamme' and 'Eventail de Madame Mallarmé' which show his complete mastery of the sonnet form. Such sonnets, whether dedicated to his wife or his mistress, represent the nineteenth-century French love sonnet at its most subtle and persuasive, challenging the translator to find equivalent solutions to the poet's seemingly effortless conflation of images of writing, movement and erotic celebration.

As with Baudelaire, the metaphysical themes of Nothingness or *Néant*, Anguish or *Angoisse* become perpetual in Mallarmé, linking his thinking to that of contemporary philosophers such as Nietzsche and Kierkegaard. The Baudelairian concern with the Ideal becomes enriched and transformed in Mallarmé by its implicit reference in such concepts as *Idéal, Idée* to the process of signification (the object to signifier, the signifier to the signified). The movement of the Idea or the Ideal is often linked to those dialectical phenomena, already mentioned (fan, wing, bird, lace, etc) which re-enact or allegorize poetic inspiration or linguistic expression (as in, for example, 'Une dentelle s'abolit').

Feuillets d'Album

'Album Leaves' shows Mallarmé as an occasional poet, though none the less subtle in his formal and linguistic moves as a sonneteer. In 'Feuillet d'album' he adopts the English or Shakespearian form of the sonnet, which allows him a greater freedom of rhyme combination (three sets of two followed by a clinching final couplet) as opposed to the quadruple repetition of two rhyme sounds followed by three of two in the regular French sonnet (as in 'Remémoration d'amis belges'). Where the shorter, octosyllabic verse line promotes a more sprightly, playful effect, the Alexandrine (or 'drapeau national' as Mallarmé calls it) promotes a more serious tone, as in the two love sonnets 'Dame sans trop d'ardeur' and 'O si chère de loin et proche et blanche'. The particular quality and challenge of the latter two poems is the elaboration of a varied but fundamentally unified set of images masterfully elaborated within the unified form of the sonnet. The necessity of finding rhymes meant that in 'Oh so dear whether near or afar', a greater degree of variety and a certain anglicization of the sonnet form was required in translation.

Chansons bas

In his 'low songs' Mallarmé at times permits himself playfully to verge on the obscene, whether, as in 'The Lavender Seller' and 'Billet à Whistler', evoking female genitalia or in 'Little Tune, warlike', the masturbatory fantasies of the poet sheltering by his fireside in Paris during Franco-Prussian war. Once again, the Shakespearian form of the sonnet is in these poems united with the hepta- or octosyllabic verse line to create an explosive bundle of fragmentary perceptions that reach their climax with a bang in the final couplet. Mallarmé referred to the latter as a 'dernière pirouette' (a last pirouette) a 'queue de comète' (a comet's tail), the task of finding convincing and spectacular equivalents to Mallarmé's rhymes being a particular challenge to the translator.

Plusieurs Sonnets

This section comprises Mallarmé's four most famous and important sonnets that together constitute a 'metaphysical' cycle that may be interpreted either as proposing—to follow the hermeneutic approach of a critic such as Richard (1961)—imaginative pathways traced by the sonnets leading from despair and anguish to the creation of meaning in the universe,—or a veiled statement and poetic celebration of the ultimate undecidability or impossibility of representation, as subsequently theorized by a deconstructive philosopher such as Derrida (1972). Whichever view is taken, the sonnets offer an almost insuperable challenge to the translator in their formal perfection, suggestive richness and profound ambiguity.

In some cases the translator is obliged to improvise equivalences for lines to which it is impossible to attribute certain meaning, in others, following Mallarmé's liberty in inventing the word 'ptyx' (in the '*Sonnet en -yx*') to rhyme with other words in '-yx', he is obliged to contrive words (such as 'rix' as an English equivalent of 'rixe') not native to the target language. In rising to such challenges, the translator is brought to the heart of the linguistic process and to the realisation, ultimately, of the impossibility of arriving at any stable or fixed form of representation. Once again, the sonnet form itself provides the translator, as it does the poet, with a temporarily immemorial paradigm within which to fix a combination of expressive or interpretative potentialities. It is the translation of the work as a sonnet rather than as language that makes the whole enterprise conceivable if not possible.

As one would expect, this sonnet cycle is rich in examples of compact formulae expressing hermeneutic or semiological equations—'Terre/mystère', 'Cygne/ (as)signe', 'coup d'aile/ blancheur', 'tombeau/flambeau', 'or/-yx'(the 'absolute' values of gold/the unknown)—that Mallarmé uses as a short-hand or algebra in attempting to formulate in compact terms a complete expression of relations between phenomena, between phenomena and language, or between meanings within language. On being obliged at times to opt between a hermeneutic and a deconstructive reading of these texts, this translation has tended to opt for the former, not because this approach is in any way more justified but merely because it is hoped that it provides a more stable initial basis for the English reader subsequently to build more elaborate and critical ulterior readings. That it is difficult to avoid 'framing' the text (in both positive and negative aspects of that verb) is in any case an important lesson to be learnt from any attempt to interpret or to translate Mallarmé's sonnets.

One such frame in which Mallarmé's work gives itself to be explored relates his preoccupations to those recurring in contemporary and subsequent voices of dissent. The reappraisal and development of the Baudelairian themes mentioned in *Autres Poëmes* reaches its apotheosis in the mature Mallarmé's simultaneously philosophical and baffling sonnets. That the newfound anxiety seizing later nineteenth-century consciousness emanated from a universe now presenting itself as *Néant* was perhaps, for Mallarmé, only a symptom of the crisis of representation ('Crise de vers'). This crisis, more profound than the disappearance of this or that form of present meaning ('God', 'Man', the 'soul'), was brought about by the dawning realization that the modes and forms by which we represent experience and existence are founded on arbitrary and contingent structures. The groundless forms of representation are both generative of experience yet remain unconcerned with the truthful representation or exposition of a totality of referents ('reality' or the 'world') exterior to the system of representation. It is verse (*vers*) for Mallarmé that, in an expanded sense, designates the appearance of structure and order, and the veiling over, of the contingent bases of representation. The crisis of representation is thus a crisis of verse insofar as verse rests on conventional, created structures; but it is a crisis to which verse, in superimposing on or finding formal order in language, and offering a semblance of necessity to representation, is also the response.

Mallarmé's work in such sonnets as formally perfect yet suggestive as these, is an attempt to salvage meaning and value not through the translation of the poem into an allegorical sense present in a clearer, more conceptual form, but through harnessing the disseminatory power of language and images to investigate potential, provisional frameworks in which meaning, order and beauty can appear. Prescient of the fundamental anxiety that would culminate in the 'linguistic turn', the motifs underlying this critical, diagnostic analysis of the *Zeitgeist* reappear in different configurations in fields other than poetry: for example, the Nietzschean critique of metaphysics undertaken in the name of creating new values, the Freudian concern with a linguistic ingenuity other to the conscious manipulation of representational systems, or the Saussurean and Structuralist insight into the differential and fractured yet structured, synchronic constitution of language, conceptuality and subjectivity.

Hommages et tombeaux

Mallarmé's *Tombeaux* are among the most satisfying sonnets he produced, combining a subtle assessment of the worth of the poets, musicians or other great men they celebrate with an ongoing reflection on what is at stake in artistic representation. The sonnet dedicated to Poe is the most famous, its lapidary formulae such as 'Tel qu'en Lui-même enfin l'éternité le change' and 'Donner un sens plus pur aux mots de la tribu', despite or because of their ambiguity, being elevated within the French tradition to the status of epigrammes. The tribute to Baudelaire, shot through with the ambivalence inherent in the nature of poison and its relation to the remedy (the antidote, the vaccination), is enthralling in its paradoxical evaluation of the poet who was incontestably Mallarmé's most important precursor. We are easily persuaded by Mallarmé that the poet of *Les Fleurs du Mal* is a salutary poison, to be breathed in though lethal, the seduction of Baudelaire's poetic language or *sorcellerie évocatoire* being as powerful as any other form of prostitution. Once again, the dilemma of translation is implicit in the interpretative process, the English rhythms attempting to match the seduction of the French, the rhymes bust/ dust attempting to clinch the combination of erotic and scabrous that colours Mallarmé's appreciation. The homage to Wagner, like the music it celebrates, at once subtle and overblown, poses similar challenges to the translator: music to words, words to words, ink silencing (in the original) or voicing (in the translation)—mirroring binds that are the stuff of Mallarmean poetry and the joy and nightmare of his translator.

Autres Poëmes et sonnets

The cycle of three sonnets that opens this section in many ways attempts to re-write in more compact terms the major issues tackled in the preceding cycle *Plusieurs Sonnets*. So the questions of the meaning of the cosmos and the poet's attempt to grasp it ('Tout Orgueil fume-t-il du soir'), the conjuring of some ultimate and ineluctable object of desire ('Surgi de la croupe et du bond'), the creation or projection of some inspirational meaningful sign ('Une dentelle s'abolit'), are re-enacted on a somewhat smaller stage, the poet's lack of room for manoeuvre resulting from his adoption of the octosyllabic verse line, each phrase or sentence needing four to six lines of verse to articulate its central proposition. Unfortunately it was impossible in the translation process to capture the capital 'O' of the setting sun embedded in the word 'Orgueil' in Sonnet I's first line, though there was more luck in Sonnet II in which 'mère/Chimère' could be matched by 'admirer/Chimera', and in Sonnet III where the Keatsian adjective 'forlorn' from the 'Ode to Melancholy' came to the rescue in line 12 so that an adequate equivalent for 'fenêtre/naître' could be found in 'sash forlorn/ might have been born'. But the ultimate test of rhyming ingenuity and metrical compactness comes in 'A la nue accablante tu' where the octosyllabic verse line is almost overwhelmed by the crushing foam of the white page, isolated lines are buffeted like flotsam on the waves—'Tout l'abîme vain éployé'—and even parentheses are turned back on themselves by the page's lateral pressure on the poem:

(tu

Le sait, écume, mais y baves).

Intertexual references to Coleridge's *Rime of the Ancient Mariner* came to the rescue in this poem, as did those from Blake's 'Jerusalem' ('desire'/ 'chariots of fire') in the sestet of 'M'Introduire dans ton histoire', the latter poem receiving the freest translation in this collection—it having been the first attempted (before a more systematic approach had been developed), the continuation of the martial imagery in Quatrain 2 betraying the translator's interest in boxing.

A final liberty may have been taken in the translation of 'Mes bouquins refermés sur le nom de Paphos' in which the unspecified whiteness suggested in Quatrain 2 may be conceived either as a wintry snow scene or—as is the case in this translation—as a continuation of the surf imagery of Quatrain 1. Once again, the disseminatory potentialities of language here provide the translator with a challenge to which he can only ever partially rise.

Bibliography

Primary Texts

Mallarmé, Stéphane *Oeuvres complètes* (ed. H. Mondor & G. Jean-Aubry, Bibliothèque de la Pléiade. Paris: Gallimard, 1945).

Mallarmé, Stéphane *Correspondance 1862–1898* (10 vols., ed. H. Mondor, J.-P. Richard, L. J. Austin. (Paris: Gallimard, 1959–1984).

Selected Translations of Mallarmé's Poems

Bosley, Keith *Mallarmé. The Poems*. (Harmondsworth: Penguin, 1977).

Carson, Ciaran *The Alexandrine Plan*. (Loughcrew: The Gallery Press, 1998).

Chadwick, Charles *The Meaning of Mallarmé. A bilingual edition of his 'Poésies' and 'Un coup de Dés'*. (Scottish Cultural Press, 1996).

Coffey, Brian (1990) *Poems of Mallarmé*. (London: The Menard Press, 1990).

Coffey, Brian (1988) *Versions of some sonnets by Mallarmé*. (Dublin: hardPressed poetry, 1988).

Hartley, Anthony *Mallarmé. Poems*. (Prose Translations) (Harmondsworth: Penguin, 1965).

Macintyre, C. F. *Stéphane Mallarmé. Selected Poems*. Berkeley, Los Angeles, London: University of California Press, 1957).

North, Christine *Mallarmé: eleven translations with the originals facing*. (Enfield: Perdita Press, 2006).

Paul, David *Poison and Vision. Poems and Prose of Baudelaire, Mallarmé and Rimbaud*. (Salzburg: University of Salzburg, 1996).

Weinfield, Henry *Stéphane Mallarmé. Collected Poems* (Berkeley, Los Angeles, London: University of California Press, 1994).

Selected Studies of Mallarmé's Poetry

Bowie, Malcolm *Mallarmé and the Art of Being Difficult* (Cambridge: Cambridge University Press, 1978).

Derrida, Jacques 'La Double Séance' in *La Dissémination*. Paris: Editions du Seuil, 1972).

Pearson, Roger *Unfolding Mallarmé: the development of a poetic art.*
(Oxford: Clarendon Press, 1996).

Pearson, Roger *Mallarmé and Circumstance: the translation of silence.*
(Oxford: Oxford University Press, 2004).

Richard, Jean-Pierre *L'Univers imaginaire de Mallarmé.* Paris:
Editions du Seuil, 1961).

Scherer, Jacques *Grammaire de Mallarmé.* Paris: Nizet, 1977).

Scott, David 'Symbolist Aesthetics: Mallarmé' in *Pictorialist
Poetics: poetry and the visual arts in nineteenth-century France,*
(Cambridge: Cambridge University Press, 1988).

Printed in the United Kingdom
by Lightning Source UK Ltd.
134135UK00001B/320/P